When the World Takes the Wind
Out of Your Sails

When the World Takes the Wind Out of Your Sails

James W. Moore

Abingdon Press
NASHVILLE

WHEN THE WORLD TAKES THE WIND OUT OF YOUR SAILS

This book is printed on acid-free paper.

Library of Congress Cataloging-in-Publication Data

Moore, James W. (James Wendell), 1938-
  When the world takes the wind out of your sails / James W. Moore.
    p. cm.
  ISBN 978-1-4267-1135-0 (book - pbk./trade pbk., adhesive - perfect binding : alk. paper)
  1. Trust in God—Christianity. 2. Christian life—Methodist authors. I. Title.
  BV4637.M57 2010
  248.4—dc22

                                                            2010037683

Scripture quotations unless noted otherwise are taken from the New Revised Standard Version of the Bible, copyright 1989, Division of Christian Education of the National Council of the Churches of Christ in the United States of America. Used by permission. All rights reserved.

The Scripture quotations noted KJV are from the King James Version.

Scripture quotations marked RSV are from the Revised Standard Version of the Bible, copyright 1952 [2nd edition, 1971] by the Division of Christian Education of the National Council of the Churches of Christ in the United States of America. Used by permission. All rights reserved.

Portions of chapter 9 previously appeared in a different form in chapter 5, "When You Feel Completely Stressed Out," in *9/11—What a Difference a Day Makes*, by James W. Moore (Nashville: Abingdon Press, 2002).

10 11 12 13 14 15 16 17 18 19—10 9 8 7 6 5 4 3 2 1
MANUFACTURED IN THE UNITED STATES OF AMERICA

For Mildred (aka GG),

who has, with the help of God,

handled the storms of life

with grace and strength

for some ninety-four years

Also for

Dale, Gary, Ashley, and June,

who continue to lovingly support her

in every way

CONTENTS

INTRODUCTION

When the World Takes the Wind Out of Your Sails

His name was Nodar Kumaritashvili. He was just twenty-one years old. The nation of Georgia was so proud of him. He was one of their most promising young athletes. They had hoped to watch him represent his country well and vie for a medal in the 2010 Winter Olympic Games in Vancouver. But, instead, they gathered on a Saturday morning to mourn his loss, after the young luger was thrown to his death in a practice run on the Olympic luge track just hours before the opening ceremonies.

Nodar lost control of his sled during a training run, shot off the course and slammed into a trackside steel pole at nearly ninety miles per hour. The following Saturday morning, thousands of mourners gathered in the yard of his family's two-story brick home in Bakuriani, Georgia, for a traditional funeral feast.

Inside the house, Nodar's body lay in a coffin, surrounded by Orthodox Christian icons, burning candles, and stunned, heartbroken family members and friends.

A small choir sang chants, and a portrait of the handsome young athlete hung on the wall.

Nodar's father, David Kumaritashvili, stared at the portrait and with tears glistening in his eyes, he said: "I wanted to throw a wedding feast for you. Instead, we have a funeral."

A few days later young Nodar Kumaritashvili was laid to rest in the cemetery of a tiny church in that beautiful mountain village where he grew up and trained for years to become an Olympian.

He was so young and so talented, with high hopes, big dreams, and great expectations. So perfectly conditioned, so full of life—and then so quickly gone!

Nodar's story is a harsh, sobering, and dramatic reminder of how hard life can sometimes be, and how fragile! The stark reality is that the tough and painful problems of life can so suddenly rise up and knock us flat. Sometimes when we least expect it, the world can take the wind out of our sails.

What do we do when that happens? What do we do when the hard knocks of life tumble in on us and threaten to tear us apart? How do we respond to the troubles of the world?

Do we try to run away and hide? Do we just quit on life, throw in the towel, feel sorry for ourselves, and wallow in self-pity? Do we retreat into a hard shell of cynicism, forever bitter and angry at the world and every-thing and everyone in it? Do we go through the rest of our life with a chip on our shoulder, ready to fight at the drop of a hat? Do we look for someone to blame it on? Do we blame it on God?

No, there is a better way, and the Scriptures remind us of that over and over again. Remember how the psalmist put it: "Yea, though I walk through the valley of the shadow of death, I will fear no evil: for thou art with me" (Psalm 23:4 KJV).

The apostle Paul knew well the problems, the chal-lenges, the dangers, and the heartaches of this world and remember how he said that nothing (not even death) "will be able to separate us from the love of God in Christ Jesus our Lord" (Romans 8:39).

The Scriptures tell us boldly and repeatedly that the good news of our faith is that God is always with us with gracious love and redeeming power. So we don't have to "run scared" through life. In our joys and sorrows from the cradle to the grave (and even beyond the grave), the good news is that God will be with us, giving us the strength we need when we need it.

So many times as a pastor, I have heard people in hard, tough circumstances say, "This is the hardest thing we have ever gone through, but we are going to make it because God is with us as never before." Notice

those last three words, "as never before." Isn't that
something? "God is with us as never before," they say.
There are probably two reasons that people feel that
way. First, when we are in those tough times, we are
more open to God's presence and help; and second,
when we are facing the hard troubles of the world, that's
when God (like a loving parent) wants to be closest to
us, his children, to help us and support us and encourage us.

That's what this book is really all about: the reminder
of God's greatest promise to never forsake us, to never
desert us, to never leave us, but to always, come what
may, be there with us and for us, even when (especially
when) the world tries to take the wind out of our sails.

CHAPTER ONE

Remember That Our Hope Is in God

SCRIPTURE: MARK 4:35-41

In January of 1983, I was privileged to visit the Holy Land for the first time. On that trip, our travel group spent two days in the city of Tiberius, which is located on the western shore of the Sea of Galilee.

To this day when I think of Tiberius, three vivid images jump quickly into my mind. First, I recall that on our first night there, a small earthquake hit nearby, sending a dramatic tremor through our hotel. Now, that will get your attention and sear itself into your memory forever.

Second, I remember being surprised by the size of the Sea of Galilee. Actually as bodies of water go, the Sea of Galilee is really rather small. It's only thirteen miles long, north to south, and only eight miles across

1

at its widest span. There are lakes in Texas that size and indeed even much larger.

Third, I remember watching a storm develop on the Sea of Galilee. It came with amazing quickness and with no warning. One minute the sun was shining brightly, the winds were calm, and the water was still as glass. But then, out of the blue, the storm sprang up. Harsh gusts of wind began to blow, and in no more than fifteen minutes the sea was white with large foam-crested waves. Great billowing waves crashed on the shoreline, and over a hundred yards from the lakeside you could feel the spray of water kicked up by the storm. In just a matter of minutes, the still, glassy water and the clear blue sky had given way to a violent, raging storm.

Mark's Gospel (in chapter 4) records just such a storm, a storm that came with frightening suddenness and intensity. It lashed against the boat that was carrying Jesus and his disciples. The disciples, "scared out of their wits," rush to Jesus for help. Of all things, can you imagine this? He was sound asleep, resting peacefully on a pillow in the stern of the ship. He was completely at peace in the midst of a storm. There must be a sermon there somewhere.

The original Greek words here are vivid and they add greatly to the drama of the story. In the original Greek text the storm is called a *seismos,* the Greek word for "earthquake." *Seismos* gives us our word "seismograph," which is the instrument we use today to record the intensity of an earthquake. The implication is that the storm in Mark 4 was like an earthquake at sea.

Another interesting Greek word here is *kaluptesthai*, which means "completely hidden." The waves were so high that the boat was "completely hidden" as the waves crested and towered over it and tossed it to and fro.

The disciples were understandably terrified by this sudden turn of events. Only moments before, Jesus had been teaching from this boat as it sat calmly in the quiet and peaceful waters, but now the boat was being hurled about violently by the mad waves of the raging sea. "Wake up, teacher, wake up," they shout to him, shaking his shoulder with panic in their eyes. And then, just a bit irritated with him for being able to sleep in such dangerous circumstances, they question him: "Don't you care? We are all about to be killed here. Are you going to sleep through this? Don't you even care?" And then in his special way, Jesus rises to the occasion. He stands up and speaks out, and he calms the storm.

When I was a young boy growing up in Memphis, Tennessee, I went to St. Mark's Methodist Church. I can remember vividly the Sunday evening services we had in that little neighborhood church. We would almost always have an informal hymn sing and sometimes the congregation would call out our "request hymns." One favorite hymn almost always called for was number 273 in the old *Cokesbury Hymnal*. It was called "Peace! Be Still!" It was based on this Scripture passage in Mark 4. Remember the words:

Master, the tempest is raging!
The billows are tossing high!
The sky is o'er-shadowed with blackness,
No shelter or help is nigh;
"Carest Thou not that we perish?"
How canst Thou lie asleep,
When each moment so madly is threat'ning
A grave in the angry deep?"

Then in the Refrain, Jesus gives his answer:

"The winds and the waves obey my will—
Peace, be still! Peace, be still!
Whether the wrath of the storm-tossed sea,
Or demons, or men, or whatever it be,
No water can swallow the ship where lies
The Master of ocean and earth and skies;
They all shall sweetly obey My will;
Peace, be still! Peace, peace be still.
They all shall sweetly obey My will;
Peace, peace, be still!"

This miracle story in Mark 4 is a powerful parable for us anytime, but especially it's relevant for us whenever we have to face the storms of life. No one of us is immune. The storms will come for all of us. We can be sure of that. And sometimes the harsh storms can knock us down and absolutely take the wind out of our sails. What do we do then? How do we get back up and make it through the storm? There are many lessons here in this powerful story in Mark 4. Let me underscore three of them. I'm sure you will think of others.

The First Lesson Here Is That Life Is Uncertain

The storm came so quickly. The situation changed so rapidly. Life is like that, isn't it? It's so uncertain. We see it again and again in the Scriptures. Like Jesus and his disciples, we can be sailing along peacefully under clear blue skies with everything looking so promising and so bright. But suddenly, so suddenly, the clouds gather, the skies darken and rumble, the winds blow, and so quickly we find ourselves caught in the fury of a storm, a storm that alarms and shakes our world.

So quickly it can happen. In the early part of the decade of the 1990s, the prospect for peace looked so promising. The Cold War had thawed, the Berlin Wall had come down. All over the world, people were so hopeful that we could finally have a lasting peace.

But then, a small defenseless nation was aggressively invaded and the Gulf War began. Innocent people far from the battlefields became the targets of SCUD missiles. In defiance of the Geneva Convention, prisoners of war became the victims of ruthless mistreatment. The earth was scorched. The environment was attacked. The gulf was contaminated. And suddenly, most of us had loved ones caught in the eye of the storm.

Just a few months earlier, our son graduated from college. When our family arrived on the university campus for the graduation exercises, one of his former roommates, a fun-loving young man, met us with a gracious offer. Our son's roommate was not graduating this time around, so he volunteered to take our video camera and to move about the arena and make a creative video tape of the graduation for us. With a warm smile, he said to us: "Now, you all find a good seat, sit down and relax and enjoy the commencement exercises and be the proud family, and I will be your camera-man." Well, he did that for us. He made the video, accompanied by his own fresh and witty narration of the big event.

At the time, he (just twenty-two years old then) was a laid-back, easy-going, free-spirited college student, having the time of his life. Just a few short weeks later, he was in a tent in the Saudi Arabian Desert, just twenty miles south of the Kuwait border. And when the ground war started, he was one of the first Marines to see action.

That young man served our country well and bravely and is safely back home now, but the point is clear and the message is important: life is uncertain, because the storms can hit so swiftly. The changes can happen so promptly. The dangers can come so rapidly. All can be so calm and peaceful and then so quickly, so forcefully, the storms can come into our lives with amazing suddenness.

That's the first lesson here: Life is so uncertain.

Now, This Leads Us to a Second Lesson—Namely, We Need to Prepare Ahead

When the storm hit, Jesus was relaxed, poised, and confident because of the deep spiritual resources he had built up ahead of time. He had prepared. We see the opposite of this in Shakespeare's play *The Tempest*. There, when the storm hit, the mariners ran to and fro shouting in desperation: "All is lost! To prayers! To prayers! All is lost! To prayers!"

You see, for them, faith was nothing more than a last ditch effort, a last resort, something you turn to only when all else fails. Not so with Jesus. For him, faith was a daily lifestyle, a way of life that conditioned him, prepared him, and gave him the spiritual strength to face the harsh storms that came his way.

A few years ago, I wrote a book titled *Noah Built His*

Ark in the Sunshine—that is, he prepared in the sunshine for the flood that was to come. The people laughed at him. They made fun of him. They told him that what he was doing was ridiculous and unnecessary. After all, the sun was shining. Why waste time building an ark? But Noah kept on building, and when the troubled waters came he was prepared, he was ready, he was equipped and able to ride out the storm.

Now, let me tell you something. We need to build an ark in the sunshine. We need to prepare ahead of time for the storms of life that will inevitably explode with fury into our lives. Somewhere down the line, maybe even when we least expect it, there is a storm waiting for you and me; and if we haven't prepared, if we haven't built up inner resources of spiritual strength, it will sweep us under.

During the Vietnam War, a friend of mine went through four horrendous years as a POW. To this day, he attributes his survival to his faith in God. He tells of the awful abuse, the torture, the cruel and inhumane treatment that he and others endured. And he remembers what gave him the courage to hold on. Over and over, he repeated those words he learned as a child in Sunday school, words he had carried through his youth, words that shaped his philosophy of life as an adult.

Yea, though I walk through the valley
of the shadow of death, I will fear no
evil: for thou art with me. (Psalm 23:4 KJV)

[Nothing] will be able to separate us from the love
of God in Christ Jesus our Lord. (Romans 8:39)

The great biblical promise of God is to always be with us. That promise kept my friend alive and sane and hopeful. The advance spiritual preparation in his life served him well and saved him in the time of storm. No question about it, life is uncertain. We need to prepare ahead to face the storms that are certain to come.

This Brings Us to the Third and Final Lesson, the Most Important One of All, Namely This: Our Hope Is in God!

When the storm hit, the disciples turned to Jesus for help, and he came through for them. Now, when we read this story in Mark 4 closely, we see that Jesus actually calmed two different storms, the one without and the one within. He stilled the storm of fury lashing at the boat, and he stilled the storm of fear raging inside the disciples.

Remember how William Barclay put it. He said, "In this story, there is something much more than just the calming of a storm at sea. That's here to be sure. But on a deeper level, the meaning of this story is that wherever Jesus is, the storms of life become calm. It means that in the presence of Jesus, the most terrible of tempests turns to peace" (William Barclay, *The Gospel of Matthew*, The Daily Study Bible Series, revised edition [Philadelphia: The Westminster Press, 1975], 318).

Barclay knew this from experience. Some years ago, as suddenly as that storm in Mark 4 came to the Sea of Galilee, a storm struck abruptly, violently, shatteringly into his life. His twenty-one-year-old daughter and her fiancé were both drowned in a yachting accident just days before they were to be married. William Barclay was crushed, devastated. He said that sudden, horrible, tragic event lashed at the very fiber of his soul.

But somehow, as never before, he knew the presence of Christ. Somehow he felt Christ with him and within him, stilling the storm in his heart, bringing confidence and strength and poise. Through that experience he learned that no matter what tempest of trouble or pain or sorrow may blow upon our lives, with Christ there is calm, there is victory, there is inner peace in stormy times. (See William Barclay's *Spiritual Autobiography* [Grand Rapids, Mich.: Wm. B. Eerdmanns, 1975], 45.)

It is significant to note that the greatest expressions of faith historically do seem to come in times of storm. Just as good parents want to be close to their children most of all when their children are hurting, even so when the harsh storms of life strike, God does seem to draw even closer to us. It's more likely that God's there close to us all along, but somehow in the storms we tune in better to God's presence and strength.

During World War II, Edward R. Murrow reported that during the toughest moment of the war, he saw a sign tacked on the side of a church. It was crudely lettered and it read: "If your knees knock, kneel on them."

So, when the storms come and the world takes the wind out of our sails, what do we do? Well, we do what the disciples did: We turn to Christ for help! We realize that our hope is in God and that he has the power to still the storms of life. But then what do we pray for? We pray for a quick and lasting peace without, and for a strong eternal peace within.

CHAPTER TWO

Remember That with God's Help You Can Bounce Back

SCRIPTURE: PSALM 23

A t one time or another, all of us have walked through the valley of the shadow of death. We have all had our hearts broken. We have all had the wind taken out of our sails by the hard troubles of the world.

1. She was in her early twenties, happily married—and she had just come home from the hospital with a new baby. (Life was wonderful. She had dreamed of having a baby girl, and now she had one.) The nursery was beautifully decorated in bright pink, celebrating this new little person, this lovely daughter who had now come into her family and her life in such a special way.

On one morning, this young mother was awakened by the loud, lusty cry of her healthy baby. She went in to feed her, change her, play with her, and love her.

After that warm and intimate time together she put her new daughter back into the crib and went into the kitchen to make a pot of coffee. Ten minutes later, she came back to the nursery to check on the baby. As soon as that young mother walked into that room, she knew something was wrong; her maternal instincts told her that something terrible was wrong. She rushed over to the baby's bed and into a nightmare experience. The baby was dead.

"Crib death" they called it. Mysteriously, tragically, for reasons unknown, the baby just died. And the hearts of two young parents were broken.

2. The telephone rang loudly in the middle of the night. The caller identified himself to me as the police chaplain. He had bad news for a family in our church. Their teenage daughter had been killed in a car wreck. We went together to tell the parents. We went, we told them, and of course, their hearts were broken.

3. The young man needed to talk to me. "It's urgent," he said. His fiancée had called off the wedding. The courtship had been going along smoothly, or so it seemed to him; the invitations had been sent, and the wedding preparations had been made. And then, out of the blue, she got cold feet, she balked, she got scared, she bailed out, saying that she wasn't sure she loved him. He was devastated, hurt, crushed, embarrassed. His

pride was dashed. His self-esteem was shaken. His self-image was knocked flat. His heart was broken.

4. She was a middle-aged woman. For more than thirty years, she and her husband had been happily married. Her whole world had been wrapped up in him. But then he was stricken with terminal cancer. He fought it bravely for six months, but then he died. And when he died, it was a blessed release for him. He had suffered enough. But for her, it meant a deep, debilitating grief that she seemed unable to shake, a dull aching loneliness; fear, confusion, guilt, and sometimes panic; no energy, no zest, no vibrancy, and no idea of what to do or how to handle her sorrow, a heart cracked across with care and sorrow, a heart broken.

Now, I could go on and on:

- the man who lost his job,
- the young teen-aged couple who got into trouble,
- the student who flunked out,
- the marriage that went on the rocks,
- the person who missed the promotion,
- the family ripped apart by a drug problem.

All of these people are in trouble, and they have at least three things in common. First, their hearts are broken. Second, they are going through the grief process.

Third, they have turned to the church for help and encouragement.

All of us have moments when we feel as if the bottom has dropped out of our world. All of us have known, somehow or other, the agonizing pain of a broken heart, and the truth is that we will know that pain again. So the questions fly fast and furious:

- How do we handle the demoralizing experiences of life?
- How do we make it through the lonesome valley of the shadow?
- How do we grieve productively and suffer creatively?
- How do we deal with the emotional and spiritual pain that accompanies a broken heart?
- And how do the resources of faith help?

Sometimes we deny the reality of the terrible thing that has happened to us; or we deny the reality of grief, implying that we should all be as tough as the characters played by John Wayne or Charles Bronson. But you see, when our world caves in, when we are hurt or disappointed or brokenhearted, a lot of emotional stuff and painful feelings start bubbling and gurgling deep within us—fear, anger, loneliness, anxiety, confusion, guilt, resentment, dread.

Now, those emotions need to come out; they need to be expressed or they will fester within and poison our souls. It's important to realize that there are constructive ways of expressing these emotions and there are destructive ways. The destructive ways we want to avoid like the plague because they can only add to the hurt—destructive things like getting drunk or drugging ourselves, punching somebody out, driving ninety miles an hour on the highway, running away, or pretending the hurts aren't there. These things don't help. They only make matters worse. They are destructive.

Now, let me list for your consideration some constructive ways of dealing with the emotional hurt and pain of the broken heart—simple ways that, with the help of God, do work.

Here they are.

First, When Your Heart Is Broken, Talk It Out

Maybe what we need most when we are hurt is a sympathetic ear, someone who cares enough to listen, encourage, support, and affirm.

My father died as a result of an automobile accident when I was twelve years old. I remember vividly the first day back at school after my dad's funeral, during recess, out on the school yard, telling my sixth grade friends about the car wreck that took my dad's life. One of them asked, "Jim, does it bother you to talk about it?" I can remember as if it were yesterday how I realized (even as a 12-year-old boy) that I needed to talk about it; I needed to reminisce, I needed to verbalize it, I needed to express it, I needed to talk it out.

Some years later, I also lost my mother in a car wreck. I wrote and preached a sermon about that experience and the accompanying grief. People asked, "How could you do that?" Well, I needed to do that. It was therapeutic for me. It helped me to talk it out. My heart was broken and I needed to talk about it.

When I first started out in the ministry, as I would work with people in grief, I thought it was my job to talk, to explain, to interpret. I thought I was supposed to give them answers. But now I do just the opposite. I let them talk, I encourage them to talk. I know now (because I have been through it personally many times) that what people in sorrow really need is a listener. So I say: "Tell me about it. Tell me what happened. Let's reminisce together about your loved one. Let's remember together his or her best qualities."

So, when your world caves in, when your heart is broken, find a friend with a sympathetic ear—and talk to them. Talk it out; it really helps.

It also helps immensely to talk it out with God. That's what prayer is. It is "friendship with God" and that's what friends do. They talk it out. So, feel free to talk to God and tell God honestly and openly and candidly what you are thinking, what you are feeling, and what you are needing. God will always be there for you and God will always hear you with love and understanding and compassion. God is the one who can hear your cries and give you the strength you need.

So, that's number one. Talk it out. Talk it out with a trusted friend and talk it out with God.

Second, When Your Heart Is Broken, Cry It Out

The headline in the morning paper read: "Tears Can Be a Beneficial Coping Tool." Two top scientists have been doing research on crying and have come to a conclusion that we in the church have known for years: that it's all right to cry. This is not weakness or selfishness. Sometimes we hear people say, "I'm such a baby to cry." Or, "I know it's selfish of me to cry, but..." Listen: It's all right to cry. It's normal. It's God's cleansing gift, a healthy way to express painful feelings. If you hit your thumb with a hammer and tears flood into your eyes, no one is going to come up and say, "You are selfish and childish to cry." No, it hurts; it's painful. Grief is like that; it hurts; deep ties have been severed. You have been wounded by your loss, and deep emotion is welling up. You need to cry it out. I'm afraid that too often today we are too quick to discourage crying, too quick to rush to the medicine chest for a tranquilizer. "Mom is upset; let's give her something to calm her down." But you see, we need to express these deep emotions. It's OK to talk it out and to cry it out.

Third, When Your Heart Is Broken, Work It Out

Please don't ever criticize a person who has gone through a grief experience for "going back to work too soon." That may be their way of dealing with their grief. Please don't ever criticize a child who is going through sorrow for wanting to go out and play. Play is their work and that may be their way of dealing with their heartache.

In moments of sorrow in my life, friends came and said, "You sit down there and we will do everything for you." They meant well and I appreciated their concern, but I couldn't do it that way.

I couldn't sit down.

I needed to be busy.

I needed to make the phone calls.

I needed to run the errands.

I needed to see about the arrangements.

I needed to work it out.

William Barclay preached the Sunday after his daughter died in a boating accident, and he said, "The saving reaction is simply to go on living, to go on working, and to find in the presence of Jesus Christ the strength and courage to meet life with steady eyes."

Some people find therapy in working it out, and in taking up the torch of their loved ones' best qualities, and keeping those qualities alive and well in this world.

We can talk it out, cry it out, work it out.

Fourth and Finally, When Your Heart Is Broken, Worship It Out

Some people in sorrow make a terrible mistake. They say, "I can't bear to come back to church yet. Let me get my act together first, and then I'll get back in church." But you see, it works just the other way. Let the church be part of the healing process.

Claim the fellowship and strength of the church. Let the church family's arms of love hold you up. Let the prayers, the gentle hugs, the casseroles, the tender handshakes support you and help you. Get back to regular church events as soon as you can. Remember that God loves you and He will bring you through the valley to the mountaintop on the other side.

A friend once told about a man sitting in his car at an intersection when another car turning onto his street side-swiped his back left fender. When the man walked back to the car that had hit him, he found a young woman sitting behind the steering wheel crying her eyes out. She said, "Oh, I'm so sorry; I can't believe I've done this. My husband's gonna kill me. We just got married and he gave me this car as a wedding gift, and already I've wrecked it. I've never had an accident before, and I don't know what to do."

The man reassured her and tried to calm her down, but then he told her that he would need her name, address, and her insurance information. She started crying again. "But I don't have any insurance information." The man said, "It's probably in the glove compartment. Let's check there." They looked and sure enough, it was there and attached to the insurance envelope was a note from her husband which read: "Honey, in case of an accident, remember that I love you and not the car."

That's something of a parable for us, isn't it? It's the good news of our faith. God says to us: "In case of an accident, in case of a broken heart, remember that I love you, and I will see you through."

CHAPTER THREE

Remember That It Is Important to Push Out of the Shallows

SCRIPTURE: LUKE 5:1-11

A good friend of mine, who was the pastor of a United Methodist church in Texas, tells an amazing story about something that happened to him some years ago that really got his attention when he was first starting out in the ministry.

The population growth of Dallas was moving rapidly and people were just flocking into neighboring areas, and my friend realized (as more and more people came into their church) that they needed to start a building program and expand quickly. He met with the architects, and they came up with a great plan that would ensure the long-range future of their church. Then he went to the bank to arrange the loan they would need. The banker wrote a number on a piece of paper and handed it to him, and then he said: "We will give you the loan if you will first raise that amount of money by such-and-such date. If you come back with one penny less than that amount, we won't even talk to you."

So the pastor and the leaders of the church went to work to raise that seed money: $500,000. And on the night before the deadline, they counted what they had raised, and they were exactly $14,000 short. My friend was so depressed. He sent everybody home, and he sat there at his desk (in the dark of the night) feeling blue and defeated. They had done everything they knew to do. They had left no stone unturned. They had worked so hard to raise that seed money, and then came the reality check: they were $14,000 short.

He sat there in his office wallowing in self-pity and feeling down in the dumps. How was he going to tell the board? How was he going to explain this to the congregation? Then, there was a loud knock at the door, and in came Phil. Now, Phil was the last guy in the world that my friend wanted to see in that moment; he didn't want to see anyone in that moment.

But in came Phil (and my friend groaned inside), "Well, Brother Mike,"—Phil insisted on always calling him *Brother Mike* even though my friend protested—"I understand we came up short on the building campaign." "Yes, Phil, we are $14,000 short, and I don't know what to do about it!" "Well, I do, Brother Mike. We are going to pray about it, Brother Mike !" My friend said, "Holding hands with a man in my office in the middle of the night is not my favorite thing to do." But Phil persisted and he began to pray fervently: "O Lord, help Brother Mike. Be with Brother Mike and give him strength. Enable Brother Mike to find this money we need so desperately for our church. Let someone out there rise up and bring Brother Mike the help he needs."

Finally, Phil finished his prayer and left. My friend sat back down and began to worry and stew and fret about what to do. About five minutes later, the phone rang. It was a doctor in the community. The doctor said, "I understand you folks are trying to raise money for a new building for your church. I'm not a member yet, but I think we need a good strong Methodist church up here, so I would like to help. I have had a good year, and I want to give some of my good fortune to some worthwhile cause and about five minutes ago it hit me: there's no better place to give money to than a church. So I have written out a check to your church and if you're going to be there I'd like to bring it to you right now."

A few minutes later the doctor arrived in the pastor's office and handed him an envelope. My friend thanked him. They visited a few minutes and then the doctor left. He opened the envelope and—are you ready for this?—there was a check in there for exactly $14,000! My friend was so excited and he grabbed the phone to call Phil, and he said, "Phil, this is Brother Mike!"

My friend now looks back at that experience as a kind of rebirth experience, which gave him a new appreciation for Phil, and a new understanding of the power of prayer. He felt so down and out, so discouraged and defeated, but then suddenly (out of the blue) he felt reborn! Have you ever had an experience like that? Actually this is precisely what we see happening to Simon, James, and John in Luke 5. Remember that scene with me:

They are professional fishermen, and we find them tired, worn, discouraged, and disappointed because they have fished all night and have come up empty. They have caught nothing at all! They are $14,000 short! Jesus is so perceptive. He sizes up the situation quickly, sees their problem, empathizes with them, and points them toward a solution. He says, "You're too shallow! Launch out into the deep and let down your nets for a catch." "But Master," Simon answers, "we have worked all night and we have caught nothing. The fish aren't biting, and we are tired and we are ready to give up and quit. But if you say so, we will give it a try."

They followed Jesus' lead, they obeyed his command, they did precisely what he told them to do: they launched out into deeper water, they let down their nets, and can you believe it? They caught so many fish that their nets began to break. They had to call other boats over to bring in all the fish! Simon was astonished by the power of the Master. He was so thankful for this amazing catch of fish, but he felt unworthy to be in the presence of such greatness. So he rushed to shore, fell at the feet of Jesus, and cried out, "Depart from me, O Lord, for I am a sinful man. I am not good enough, I am not worthy to be in your company." But Jesus lifted Simon up and he called him to discipleship. "Come, Simon, and follow me. I will give you a new start, a new mission, a new dream, a new life, a new birth. Follow me and I will make you a fisher of people." And Simon and James and John left everything and followed him.

Isn't that a wonderful story? There are so many things here we could talk about:

- The miracle catch;
- The call to discipleship;
- The significance of the seashore;
- The absence of Simon's brother Andrew (where is he? Why is he not in the story?);
- The importance of obedience;
- The importance of doing precisely what the Master tells us to do;

- The unique elements of this story as it's recorded here in Luke 5, elements not found in Matthew, Mark, or John;
- That sense of unworthiness that Simon felt in the powerful presence of Jesus.

All of these are important and they deserve our thought, but for now I want us to be very personal and realize that we all need to launch out into the deep and discover the new birth that comes as Christ takes us out of the shallows into the depths of life and faith and prayer. His word to us right now rings loud and clear. Can you hear him? Can you? Can you hear him calling your name and saying, "Launch out into the deep! You've been in the shallows long enough. Push out into the deep and find new life!" Let me be more specific with these three thoughts.

First, We Can Launch Out into the Depths of Gratitude

When Simon saw that incredible catch of fish Christ had blessed them with, he was filled to overflowing with gratitude. I can just hear him saying with the psalmist:

Bless the LORD, O my soul;
and all that is within me
bless his holy name!

Bless the LORD, O my soul
> and do not forget all his benefits. (Psalm 103:1-2)

That is the song of genuine thanksgiving and yet so often the song goes unsung, doesn't it? We have so much to be thankful for and yet the truth is we do forget God's goodness. We do take for granted his blessing. We do become unmindful of his generosity.

The noted journalist John Gile writes about this in his book *Keeping First Things First*. He says:

> My four-year-old daughter has a magic body. I told her so. And it's true. A few days ago she fell off a swing in a friend's yard and cut her hand. It didn't require major medical attention, just a quick washing, a small bandage, routine tear drying, and a few reassuring hugs. But today we noticed something remarkable: the cut was gone, vanished without a trace. Somehow—like magic—her body had repaired the injured hand, making it like new again.
>
> I know some cynics will come along and tell us it's not magic. They'll tell us that there's a Latin term for it and proceed to give us a boring description of the process. But that doesn't take away the magic. It just explains how God makes "magic" things happen. Our trouble is that sometimes we're too dull to recognize God's magic. Imagine if someone made a car that repaired its own dented fenders and scratched paint. The whole world would be excited about it. It would be featured on the news and make headlines around the

world. But God gives us a magic body and we just take it for granted—as we do with so many of his gifts. Lord, please forgive us for being so dull, why are we so slow to recognize and trust you, the one behind it all? (John Gile, *Keeping First Things First*, [Rockford, Ill.: JGC, 1990], 10, 64)

If we want a new lease on life, a new start, a new beginning, a new birth, a new zestfulness, a new power in prayer, one place to find that is out there in the depths of gratitude. If we will reach out and take hold of Christ's hand, he will lead us out into the deeper waters of thankfulness.

Second, We Can Launch Out into the Depths of Penitence

First Simon felt gratitude and then penitence. He was so awed and astonished by the amazing power of Jesus that he felt unworthy to be in his presence. Like Moses at the burning bush, he wanted to take off his shoes because he knew he stood on holy ground. Like Isaiah in the Temple, he felt like an unclean man with unclean lips dwelling in the midst of an unclean people. So, in anguish Simon cried out: "Go away from me, Lord, for I am a sinful man." Look at this: Simon was rocked to the depths of his soul. In the powerful presence of Christ, he felt sorrow and sadness for his sinfulness. He felt unclean and unworthy. It was the cry of penitence.

In the Scriptures, penitence is a painful process, a deeply moving experience. People cry and tear their clothes and fall on their knees and change their ways. But today (more often than not) the truth is that we treat sin so lightly and just play around in the shallows of penitence. For example, a few years ago, a writer named A. J. Langguth wrote a story about a brazen young woman who felt that she was possessed by seven demons. She is brought before Jesus for healing. Jesus looks at her for a moment and then he says, "I can help you. I can cast out those seven demons. Would you like that?" To which the young woman says, "Would you mind just casting out six?" (*Jesus Christs* [New York: Harper & Row, 1968]).

We understand that woman, don't we? There's something about all of us that wants to hold something back, that doesn't want to let go and release ourselves completely, that wants to repent and be a Christian to a point, but not beyond that point. So much of our penitence is halfhearted and shallow.

We are so much like the man who became so irate and upset when the neighborhood children walked in his freshly poured, concrete drive. He was livid. Finally, his wife said to him, "Why are you so angry? I thought you loved children." "I do love children," he said, "but I love them in the abstract and not in the concrete!" Too often, we repent in the abstract; we don't become concrete enough. Penitence means being so sorry for our sins that we change completely.

The Hebrew word for "repent" in the Old Testament is *hashivenu*, and it means "about face," "turn around," "change your direction." If we want a new life, a new start, a new beginning, a powerful prayer life, one place to find that is out there in the depths of penitence. Christ helps us launch out into the depths of gratitude and into the depths of penitence.

Third, We Can Launch Out into the Depths of Commitment

Simon, James, and John left everything and followed Jesus, and their commitment was so deep that they turned the world upside down—or maybe better put, right side up. When you stop to think about it, shallow commitment is not worth much at all, but deep commitment is one of the most powerful things in the world.

This is beautifully portrayed by a young soldier who was brought into a field hospital with an arm that had been badly shattered. The surgeon had to amputate the arm at the elbow. When the young soldier came out of the anesthesia, the surgeon told him as gently as he could, "Son, I am sorry, but we had to take your arm." The soldier (although groggy and weak) still was able to say, "Sir, you did not take it. I gave it!" That's commitment, isn't it?

I can just picture in my mind that scene from church tradition where Simon Peter is being taken out by the Romans to be executed because of his allegiance to Christ. "Crucify me upside down," Simon says. "I'm not worthy to be sacrificed like my Lord." The centurion says, "But Simon, if you will deny Christ right now, we won't have to take your life. You will be spared." Simon answers, "You are not taking my life. I'm giving it!" That's what commitment is: it's self-giving. It's the giving of ourselves in complete devotion to Christ.

Are you committed like that? Is your commitment that deep? Our Lord's word for us today is something we all need to hear and respond to in faith and obedience. Launch out into the deep; get out of the shallows. Launch out into the depths of gratitude and penitence and commitment. And listen! That is precisely how we pray—with gratitude, thanking God for all he has done for us; with penitence, confessing to God that we have not done all we could do, and asking God to help us do better; and with commitment, saying obediently to God, "Here we are, Lord, use us as the instruments of your love and peace. Enable us to do your will! Enable us to be your church. Enable us, come what may, even when the world takes the wind out of our sails, to be your faithful disciples."

CHAPTER FOUR

Remember That There Is Amazing Power in the Cross

SCRIPTURE: MATTHEW 16:24-26

Recently I ran across a story that absolutely amazed me, and yet it's a story that may well represent the "cater-culture, give-'em-what-they-want world" in which we now live. A church wanted to improve attendance at their major worship services, so they hired a powerful advertising agency to come in, study their situation, and make recommendations.

The ad agency did their research and then suggested to the church that they should get rid of all the crosses in the church because the crosses might send a negative message to prospective young worshipers!

Now, I'm sure that in its history, that advertising agency had come up with some brilliant ideas, but in my opinion, that was not one of them! We can't get rid of the cross! We don't want to get rid of the cross. The cross is the dramatic symbol of our faith, hope, love, and forgiveness. The cross is the powerful reminder of God's sacrificial and redemptive love for us. And the cross is the constant signal to us of how God wants us to live and love today, as sacrificial servants. We are not called to be prima donnas. We are called to be servants. We are called to take up the mission of Christ and to emulate the servant spirit of our Lord.

Have you heard about the man who went up to Alaska? After he had been there for a few months, he ran into a priest and said, "Father, I hate to tell you this, but I've lost my faith in God and the power of prayer." "Why is that, my son?" the priest asked politely. "Because," said the man, "a few weeks ago while hunting in the Alaskan wilderness, I became separated from my friends. It was terrible! I was out there all alone. I was in danger of freezing to death. So I prayed and prayed to the Lord to save me, but nothing happened." The priest was perplexed, and he said, "But you are here now telling me this story, so obviously you were rescued." "Oh, yes," the man said, "but the Lord had nothing to do with it. I was saved by one of the locals!"

Well, millions of us are saved by "locals," and sadly, all too often we are blind and we do not see the hand of God in it. The point is that God chooses to work through people—through Samaritans, through maidens and shepherds, through fishermen and tentmakers and missioners. The Bible makes it crystal clear that God does much of His best work through regular folks, folks like you and me.

Jesus knew this well, and that's why he called disciples to follow him, to learn from him, and ultimately to take up the torch of his self-giving and sacrificial love. And he taught his disciples that the way to do it, the way to be God's servants, is to not arrogantly grab for the crown, but rather to humbly choose the way of the cross.

We see this in Matthew 16 (one of the mountain-peak moments in all of Scripture) where he says to his disciples, and indeed to us: *"If you would come after me, first deny yourself, then take up your cross and follow me."*

No crown offered here, only a cross. No throne offered here, only a task. No mantle offered here, only a ministry. No scepter offered here, only sacrificial service. These were not just high-sounding words that Jesus was speaking into the air, this call to service and sacrifice; he meant it! He showed us he meant it, on a cross!

This is the message of the Christian faith, isn't it? Jesus chose not the way of the crown, but rather the way of the cross. And listen! That's the spirit in which he wants us to live. He calls us to follow his lead and to choose the way of the cross—a cross, not a crown.

Now, what does that mean for you and me here and now? Many things, of course, but for now let me suggest just a few of them.

First of All, to Choose the Way of the Cross Means to Take Up the Cross of Christlike Values

Let me ask you something. How do you determine the value of something? How do you decide what is really valuable? For many years now, we in America have been highly "success-conscious" and "success-oriented." And most have agreed with the definition in Webster's dictionary: "*Success* is the attainment of wealth and fame."

Now think about it. Is that success? Isn't it true that when we think of success, we immediately pull out names like Rockefeller, Ford, DuPont, and Gates? They symbolize the "sweet smell of success." But Webster was wrong. Money and fame are not enough. Those who have risen to the top of the heap are sometimes the most miserable. Their success is often a sham, because, you see, there is more to successful living than eating well and counting wealth and wearing crowns.

Our customary standards of measuring success and value are so shoddy. How much money do you make? How many cars do you have? When was the last time you had breakfast in Paris, my dear? The very questions

reflect a poverty of soul and a shallowness of understanding.

For the moment, let's forget those selfish, shallow,
superficial values and telescope in on Jesus. In him, we
see a whole new and refreshingly different understanding of what success is. His approach startles us. It's so
different. He says, *"Those among you who would be great
or successful, let them be servants."* "Let them be servants?"
What on earth can Jesus mean by that? Successful people aren't servants; successful people *have* servants!" we
cry out. What is Jesus trying to do here, upset our whole
scale of values?

Yes! That is precisely what he is trying to do. He is
giving us a whole new scale of values, a new measuring
stick, a new standard for measuring value and success.
And he says to us discipleship is better than dollars;
service is better than securities; choosing the way of the
cross is better than grasping for crowns.

There is a true story that comes from the sinking of
the *Titanic*. A frightened woman found her place in a
lifeboat which was about to be lowered into the frigid
waters of the North Atlantic on that tragic April night
of 1912. The woman suddenly thought of something
she needed, so she asked permission to return to her
stateroom before they cast off. She was told that she
could have only three minutes, otherwise, they would

have to leave without her; and she could only bring back one thing.

The woman ran across the deck which was already slanted at a dangerous angle. She hurried through the room where people had been taking bets. Everywhere she looked, she could see money floating in the ankle-deep water. She ignored it and rushed on to her room. There she reached for her jewelry box which contained her diamond rings and her expensive bracelets, her necklaces and other priceless jewelry. But then suddenly, her eyes fell on another box—a box which contained a few apples and three small oranges. She could only take one box back to the lifeboat, and the clock was ticking. Which one should she choose? What would you have done? Which one would you have chosen? The jewels or the fresh fruit? The crown or the cross? The priceless gems or the food to save lives in a lifeboat?

The woman quickly made her choice. She pushed the jewel box aside, grabbed the box with the apples and oranges, and ran back to the lifeboat and got in.

Fascinating, isn't it? Thirty minutes before, that woman would never have chosen a box of fruit over even the smallest diamond. But that life situation suddenly changed her perspective and gave her a new way of looking at things, a new way of measuring value, a new way of deciding what is important.

When we in faith accept Jesus Christ into our lives as Lord and Savior, He changes our perspective like that. He gives us a new vision, a new wisdom, a new stance, new priorities, a new way of deciding what is really valuable. He shows us how to choose the cross of service over the crown of riches.

First, to go the way of the cross means to take up the cross of Christlike values.

Second, It Means to Take Up the Cross of Christlike Love

I knew of a bright and dedicated young Christian who studied hard and long to become a Wycliffe Bible linguist. He went as a missionary to South America to help translate the Bible into the native language of the locals. But a terrible tragedy struck. He was kidnapped by hostile rebels. For no reason, they shot him and left his body in a hijacked bus.

Imagine how his parents and loved ones and coworkers must have felt at the senseless death of this devoted young man. But a year later, as a demonstration of Christian love and international good will, the churches and civic groups in his home area back in America gave an ambulance to the country where this young man had been killed. His parents traveled there for the presentation of the ambulance.

At the ceremony, his mother said, "We serve the Christ who taught us to love unconditionally.... So we come to present this ambulance as a symbol of our Christian love and forgiveness. We are able to do this because God has taken the hatred from our hearts."

Now, let me ask you something. Could you have done that? Could you forgive like that? Could you love like that? That's the way of the cross, the way of Christlike love. To choose the way of the cross means to take up the cross of Christlike values and Christlike love.

Third and Finally, It Means to Take Up the Cross of Christlike Commitment

Have you heard the story about the man who landed a job painting the yellow line down the center of the highway? This he had to do by hand. After three days the foreman called him in and said, "I don't know what's going on with you, but each day your work is slacking off. Your first day out, you did great. You painted that line for three miles. Your second day wasn't bad. You painted two miles. But today you only painted one mile. Could you explain that? Could you tell me why your work fell off each time out?" "Yes, sir. It's not my fault," said the man. "Every day I got further away from the paint can!"

Some people are like that in their faith pilgrimage. Each day they move further and further away from

God, and life becomes increasingly more difficult and burdensome.

I heard about an Anglican bishop who was asked to speak at a Christian conference in England. For many weeks he did not respond to the invitation. Finally, the conference director wrote this insistent note: "Please, Bishop, we must know if you are coming. We need to make our plans." The bishop wrote back that he was waiting for the guidance of the Holy Spirit on the matter, and he would let them know his decision in four weeks. The exasperated director fired back this letter: "Bishop, please don't bother. Cancel the invitation. We are really not interested in having anyone speak at our conference who lives four weeks away from the Holy Spirit."

Christlike commitment is a close daily walk with God. When we study the life of Jesus carefully, we see his incredible commitment to stay close to his Father and to do the will of his Father. "Thy will be done" was the watchword of his life. Total commitment, total dedication, total consecration; that's what it means to choose the way of the cross.

The hymn writer put it like this:

Take my life and let it be
consecrated, Lord, to thee.
Take my moments and my days;
let them flow in ceaseless praise.

Take my hands, and let them move
at the impulse of thy love.
Take my feet, and let them be
swift and beautiful for thee.

Take my voice, and let me sing
always, only, for my King.
Take my lips, and let them be
filled with messages from thee.
Take my silver and my gold;
not a mite would I withhold.
Take my intellect, and use
every power as thou shalt choose.

Take my will, and make it thine;
it shall be no longer mine.
Take my heart, it is thine own;
it shall be thy royal throne.
Take my love, my Lord, I pour
at thy feet its treasure store.
Take myself, and I will be
ever, only, all for thee.
(Frances R. Havergal, "Take My Life and Let It Be,"
United Methodist Hymnal, 1989, 399)

CHAPTER FIVE

Remember That We Can Trust God and Go Forward

SCRIPTURE: EXODUS 14:5-15

Some time ago, when Lou Holtz was the head football coach of the Arkansas Razorbacks, he said something we can all relate to as he spoke about the troubles we have to face in the living of these days. He said, "I know God doesn't send us more trouble than we can handle, but sometimes I think he overestimates my ability!"

I suppose we all feel that way at times. Moses and the people of Israel must have felt like that when they were caught between the Pharaoh's powerful pursuing army and the Red Sea.

Remember how Moses experienced the presence of God in a burning bush and felt called through that dramatic encounter to go to Egypt to bring the people of

Israel out of slavery and into freedom and the promised land. Remember how reluctant Moses was to take on this difficult task. He was not overjoyed with the prospect of facing the Egyptian Pharaoh and telling him to "let my people go." You could lose your head talking like that to an Egyptian king. Moses knew this was a dreadful task. To face the Pharaoh was fearsome enough. But to get him to go along with the idea of freeing the Israelite slaves was well nigh impossible—and Moses knew it. Moses was hesitant at first, but God said, "Go, Moses, and tell Pharaoh to set my people free! Go, Moses, and I will go with you."

So Moses went forward, not sure how this was going to turn out, but trusting God to be with him. Then, remember how, after a series of confrontations and conferences and dialogues and debates and plagues, finally the Pharaoh gave in. He gave the Israelites their freedom. Quickly, Moses rallied them, and led them out of Egypt and out of slavery.

The people of Israel were filled with joy. This was a historic moment for them. This was their Exodus, their deliverance, their salvation. But then as they made camp at the Red Sea, they looked back. On the horizon they saw a huge cloud of dust. As they listened they heard the unmistakable rumble of chariots and horses and soldiers. They knew what it meant! Pharaoh had changed his mind. It was Pharaoh's army coming after them, to recapture them or to kill them. The people of Israel realized their great problem. They were scared to death, because they were trapped, pinned in, cornered, "caught between the Pharaoh's army and the deep Red Sea."

Interestingly, in this dramatic story in the book of Exodus, as we read between the lines, we can see several different ways in which people try to respond to trouble. Let's look at these because they still seem to be the ways people deal with trouble today, and we just might find ourselves somewhere in the story.

If somehow we could get into a time capsule and go back in time to that scene beside the Red Sea and listen in, just as the Israelites realize that they are in big trouble and as they begin to deal with their problem, we might well overhear something like this—the classic responses to trouble.

First of All, Some Would Say, "Let's Go Back Where We Were"

"Let's go back to the good old days. What have you done to us, Moses? Why did you have to go and bring us out of Egypt? Why didn't you let us alone, and let us serve the Egyptians? Things weren't so bad back there. What we had was a lot better than being trapped out here. This is a strange, scary place. Let's go back!"

A few years ago I was in a workshop one summer at Lake Junaluska in North Carolina. The workshop leader was a nationally known writer and consultant, Dr. Lyle Schaller. One morning he put before us a fascinating question: "What is the single most powerful influence in the decision-making process? For example, if you are in a group, and you are trying to make a decision about something, or trying to plan an event or a course of action, what is the most powerful influence in the room?"

How would you answer that? Well, we discussed it for a while, and several interesting answers emerged. But then Dr. Schaller gave us his answer. He said, "No question about it, the most powerful influence in decision-making *is the past*."

He is right on target. Think about that for a moment. If you are in a group and you are trying to decide something and you are having difficulty deciding, what do you do? Well, you ask, "What did we do last year?" And nine times out of ten you do the same thing over again.

When in doubt, what do we do? We go back. We back off. We go back to the familiar! We go back to the good old days, totally forgetting that "the good old days" had their share of problems.

Isn't that the way some people face trouble? Afraid to stand up to the challenge, they want to retreat, to go back to where they were. I can imagine that that day by the Red Sea some cried, "Let's go back where we were"—but then another group cried out a second response.

Some Would Say, "Let's Run Away and Hide!"

This ploy is as old as the Garden of Eden. As soon as Adam and Eve had a problem, what did they do? They tried to run away and hide. People are still trying to do that, aren't they? People are still trying to run away from their problems and hide behind their "escapism crutches." But you can't really hide from trouble. The Israelites certainly couldn't hide thousands of people in the desert.

During the Civil War, at the Battle of Shiloh, a Union soldier from Ohio was wounded, shot in the arm. His captain saw that he was injured and barked out an order: "Gimme your gun, Private, and get to the rear!" The private handed over his rifle and ran back to the north seeking safety. But after covering two or three hundred yards, he ran upon another skirmish. Then he ran to the east and happened upon another part of the battle. Then he ran west, and encountered more fighting there. Finally he ran back to the front lines and shouted: "Gimme my gun back, Cap'n. There isn't any rear to this battle!"

Precisely. When it comes to the troubles of this world, there ain't no rear to the battle! You can't really run away and hide. To take it a step further, I can just imagine that there was still a third response to trouble at the Red Sea.

Don't You Imagine That Some Said, "Let's Lie Down and Feel Sorry For Ourselves!"

This is the way many people choose to deal with their problems. They just quit on life and give in to self-pity. They have no energy left over to use on rising to the occasion to deal with their problems creatively because they are expending all their energy crying, "Woe is me," and feeling sorry for themselves.

A couple of years ago an Atlanta newspaper ran a human interest story about a young mother who was trying to give some liquid medicine to her two-year-old son. She had put him in a high chair and the medicine in a spoon, and she was trying to get him to take his medicine. The two-year-old would not cooperate. He would shut his mouth tightly and shake his head from side to side and hit the spoon with both hands. The young mother tried and tried, but to no avail. He would not cooperate. She coaxed, she pleaded, she threatened, she bribed, but nothing worked. He would not take his medicine! Finally, tired out and worn down, the young mother gave in to self-pity. She threw the spoon down, ran out of the room crying, fled into her bedroom, and fell across the bed, sobbing.

In a few minutes, though, she heard loud laughter coming from the kitchen. It was her two-year-old son laughing delightedly. Curious, she went to investigate, and found that Grandmother had solved the problem. She had mixed the medicine with orange juice, put it into a spray bottle, and was squirting it into the mouth of the little boy.

We have only so much energy. If we use up our energy on self-pity, we won't have any left over for creative solutions.

I can imagine still a fourth response to trouble at the Red Sea.

Some Would Have Said, "Let's Find Someone to Blame"

Isn't it interesting how, when something goes wrong, the first thing we want to do is find someone to blame it on! Look at the Israelites at the Red Sea. They see that cloud of dust on the horizon being kicked up by Pharaoh's army, and immediately they turn on Moses. Moments ago, he was their champion, their leader, their hero, but now when trouble rears its head, they go for the jugular. "It's all your fault, Moses! A fine mess you've gotten us into. Why did we ever listen to you? You're the one to blame for this."

Some years ago I had a poignant experience working with an alcoholic. He had been drunk and missing for thirty-eight days. He had left home drunk on Christmas Eve, and he staggered back home on January 31. His wife called me and asked me to go to the house and check on him. When I knocked on the door, I heard a lamp crash to the floor inside. He was stumbling and falling around in a drunken stupor. I knocked again and called out his name. I heard him fall to the floor and begin crawling toward the front door. He fumbled around with the door knob and finally pushed the door open.

Can you imagine this: as the door opened, he was lying on his stomach on the floor, and he saw my feet. Slowly he turned his head upward and he found himself looking into the face of his minister. I guess at that moment, I must have looked ten feet tall to him, because he was dirty, covered with the filth of his own drunkenness, and he had not washed or shaved or changed clothes for over a month.

He began to cry. I helped him up and got him on the couch. I washed his face with a warm washcloth and began to try to get some food and coffee into him. All of a sudden, he turned on me. He blamed me for his problem. Then he blamed his wife, and then his parents. Then he started in on his neighbors and those "hypocrites down at the church." He blamed the mayor, the President, and the Congress. He even cursed God for letting him be born. And I listened.

Then, he turned back to me and said, "Aren't you going to say anything?" I answered, "Well, I was just trying to think if there is anybody else we could think of to blame this on."

He looked at me angrily, and for a moment I thought I had gone too far. But then he looked down at his feet, and after a few moments of silence, he said, "It's all my fault! I've made such a mess of my life, haven't I?" "Well," I answered, "you are a mess right now, but your life is not finished; you can start over again." He paused for a moment and said, "Jim, do you really believe that? Do you really believe that God can help me whip this thing?" And I said to him, "I surely do, but the real question is, do you believe it, and are you ready to do something about it? Are you ready to admit that you've got a problem and that you need help?"

Evidently he was, because we got him professional help. We got him to AA and now—with their help, with his church's help, with his family's help, and with God's help—he is winning the battle. He called me the other day. He hasn't had a drink in over eighteen years. He is serving this year as chairman of the board of his church and as a UMYF youth counselor.

Now he knows that he still has a problem. He is one drink away from big trouble. But he also knows that he can't blame anybody else anymore and that when he takes responsibility for his own life, his community will help him, his family will help him, his church will help him, and God will help him, too.

Now, one final response to trouble remains to be listed—the response of Moses.

Moses Said, "Let's Go Forward Trusting God"

Though caught between the Pharaoh and the deep Red Sea, Moses did not give up, he did not quit, he did not throw in the towel. No, he trusted God and went forward.

When trouble suddenly erupts into our lives, we can remember Moses at the Red Sea. He didn't have all the answers, but he did stay in communication with God. And he went forward, did the best that he knew to do, and trusted God to bring it out right.

Many years ago, I was visiting one Sunday evening in an African American church, and I was so moved and impressed by the prayer of the minister. He was an older man, and he had evidently just recently gone through some kind of trouble. I can still remember his prayer as if I heard it yesterday: "Dear Lord, we thank you for being with us during this difficult time. When Moses and the children of Israel were caught at the Red Sea, you didn't lead them over it or around it or under it. You led them *through* it. And now in the same way, when we are in trouble, you don't lead us over it or around it or under it. No, Lord, you lead us through it, and we thank you for that. We thank you, Lord, for our deliverance." And he said "Amen" and sat down. I said "Amen" in my heart.

My hope and prayer for us is that when trouble comes, we will remember Moses at the Red Sea and be strengthened by that. We will be able to go forward, trusting God to be with us and to bring it out right.

CHAPTER SIX

Remember That Easter Has Good News for You

SCRIPTURE: MATTHEW 28:1-6

A few years ago, there was an eye-catching ad in a Milwaukee, Wisconsin, newspaper's classified section. In big bold letters the headline of the ad read: "USED TOMBSTONE." Underneath the headline were these words: "Used Tombstone for Sale. Real bargain for someone named 'Dingo.' Call for more information."

Wouldn't you just love to know the rest of that story? Who in the world was this person named Dingo—and why did he or she no longer have need for a tombstone? The image of a "used tombstone" may at first glance seem somber or depressing. But think of it again: A used tombstone means that its previous owner no longer has any use for it, doesn't need it anymore. It has become a cast-off, an unnecessary item.

This is precisely what the Easter story is all about. The message is clear: the tomb is empty! The stone marker is no longer needed! Jesus Christ has conquered death. Good Friday wasn't a period, wasn't an exclamation point; it was only a comma. The story wasn't finished; the battle wasn't over! Jesus has the last word! Jesus has the victory! Jesus Christ is risen!

Remember the story with me. On the Thursday night before Easter, Jesus was arrested on false charges. He was brutally beaten, rushed through a fixed trial held illegally in the middle of the night, and was declared guilty. The next day, Good Friday, Jesus was crucified and then he was buried in a borrowed grave. And then on Easter Sunday morning Mary Magdalene trudged in sorrow to the tomb looking for a dead body and found instead a risen Lord. She then ran shouting the good news of Easter to the others: "I have seen the Lord! I have seen the Lord! He is risen!" That night, Easter Sunday night, the disciples gathered behind closed doors to try to figure out what this all meant. Should they believe Mary? Had she really seen him? Had he really been resurrected from the dead? They wanted to believe, but it seemed too good to be true.

Then suddenly the risen Lord was with them in that very room. "Peace be with you," he said to them. "Don't be afraid." "It's all right." "I'm here." He showed them his hands and his side, and they were filled with joy and relief. And then he said to them, "As the Father sent me so I send you." He then breathed on them and said: "Receive the Holy Spirit!" All the disciples were there. All, that is, except Thomas. A week later, the risen Lord returned to reassure and redeem doubting Thomas.

Now, in this amazing story we see neatly outlined three of the great gifts of Easter, three incredible gifts Easter gives to us. Here they are: Easter gives us a great comfort, a commission, and companionship. Let's take a look at these together.

First, Easter Gives Us a Great Comfort

Easter gives us a comfort and consolation when our hearts are heavy. Those disciples were grieving, they were afraid, they were disillusioned. Their hearts were broken. They were filled with despair and confusion and guilt. And then the risen Lord came bringing comfort and consolation and hope: "Be at peace," he said. "Don't be afraid anymore." It's OK. I'm here with you. Death thought it had the last word at Golgotha, but as it turns out we have the last laugh.

Some years ago, my friend Rod Wilmoth wrote a wonderful piece titled the "Laughter of Easter." In it, he said,

There are some marvelous pictures that come out of the Resurrection stories. Can't you just imagine Mary getting together with Jesus later and saying with laughter, "I thought You were the gardener."

Or try to imagine those two men walking on the Emmaus Road . . . laughing later with Jesus and saying, "Just think, we were trying to tell You about the One who had died."

It does not end there. Remember how Sir Thomas More . . . joked with the hangman on the way to the gallows because his conscience was clear. He knew he was serving God. He could laugh and joke and smile as he faced death because he knew death was not the end. . . . "O death, where is they sting?" (Rod Wilmoth, March 31, 1991)

A good friend of mine tells about a delightful experience he had some years ago. He was on vacation in England and went one night to see Shakespeare's play *A Midsummer Night's Dream* in Stratford-on-Avon, which, of course, is the home of William Shakespeare, just outside of London. My friend said what made it a memorable experience was that the play featured the distinguished actor Charles Laughton. Laughton played the role of Bottom, the chief comic character in the play. My friend described what happened in the play that night like this:

In one scene Bottom is supposed to die. Oh my goodness . . . did Charles Laughton ever die! You thought that Charles Laughton would never finish the death scene.... He really knew how to die. He went on and on. He was finally lying on the stage with his chest and stomach resembling an enormous tide of ebbing and flowing just going up and down.... You were gasping with him and you thought, "Will he ever stop?" Finally Bottom died. Charles Laughton played the part so well that the audience applauded. I love what Charles Laughton did.... He got up and took a bow!

We can only imagine the response that produced!

They crucified Jesus. They killed him, and yet I can tell you that on that first Easter Sunday, Jesus stepped out of that tomb and took a bow! And because of the Resurrection of our Lord, we know as Christians that you and I will be able to do the same thing when we die. This is the good news of our faith, the good news of Easter. This is our comfort and consolation when things are tough and life is hard and our hearts are heavy.

Sometimes the Good Fridays we face in this life threaten to do us in and bury us, but then along comes Easter to remind us that God will ultimately win. Goodness will ultimately win. Truth and Love will ultimately win! At Calvary, evil had its best chance to defeat God and couldn't do it. God won. That's the joy of Easter, and through faith in him the victory can be ours as well! If that doesn't give us strength for the hard times, I don't know what will.

The first gift of Easter is the gift of a great comfort.

Second, Easter Gives Us a Great Commission

The risen Lord returned to put the disciples to work, to pass them the torch, to give them a job. Remember Margaret Deeney's poem called "The Greatest Words," which most people would assume to be "I love you." Listen to what the poet says:

> But the greatest words in all the world
> Are . . . I've got a job for you!
> (*Leaves of Gold* [Fort Worth, Tex.: Brownlow, 1995])

The good news of the Christian faith is that that's exactly what God says to us—yes, to you and me—"I've got a job for you! You are important to me! You are valuable! You are needed! I have something I want you to do for me that no one else can do. I want to put you to work."

Here's how the risen Lord says it to the disciples of old—and to you and me today. He says: "As the Father has sent me, so I send you" (John 20:21). In other words: Take up the cross! Take up the torch! Take up my ministry! Give yourself in sacrifice and service as I have given myself!

There is a fascinating story about Abraham Lincoln during the time of his presidency. On many Wednesday evenings, he would go to hear the preaching at the New York Avenue Presbyterian Church near the White

House. Lincoln was leaving the service one night when one of his assistants asked him, "Mr. Lincoln, what did you think of the sermon tonight?" Lincoln thought for a moment, and then he said, "Well, the content was excellent. And Dr. Gurley spoke with great eloquence. It was obvious that he had put a great deal of work into that sermon." "Then you thought it was a great sermon, Mr. President?" "No, I did not say that." "But sir, you said it was an excellent sermon." Lincoln replied, "No, I said the content was excellent and that the preacher spoke with eloquence. But Dr. Gurley on this night forgot one important matter—He forgot to ask us to do something great!"

Jesus didn't make that mistake, did he? He asks us to do something great. He asks us to do the greatest, most important thing in the world—to take up his ministry of sacrificial love. "As the Father has sent me [to give myself for you]," he said, "even so I send you [to give yourself for others]" (John 20:21).

First, Easter gives us comfort; and second, Easter gives us a great commission.

Third and Finally, Easter Gives Us a Great Companionship

Easter gives the promise of God's constant and continuing presence with us in all the circumstances of life.

In John 20:22, Jesus promises the gift of the Holy Spirit to always be with us and to always watch over us. Remember how it reads: "He breathed on them and said to them, 'Receive the Holy Spirit.'"

Many years ago, Julia Ward Howe was talking to Charles Sumner, the distinguished senator from Massachusetts. She was telling him about one of his constituents who needed his help and encouraging him to get involved in helping this person. The senator answered with a tone of exasperation: "Julia, I am a United States senator. I've become so busy I can no longer concern myself with individuals and their problems." To that, Julia Ward Howe said, "Charles, that is really quite remarkable. Even God himself hasn't reached that stage."

Indeed he hasn't. God cares about you and me personally. He knows your name and mine. He knows our joys and sorrows, our defeats and victories, our agony and our ecstasy. He knows our prayers before we even pray them. He is nearer to us than breathing. The hymn-writer put it like this:

> Now let the heavens be joyful!
>   Let earth the song begin!
> Let the round world keep triumph,
>   and all that is therein!
> Let all things seen and unseen

their notes in gladness blend,
for Christ the Lord hath risen,
    our joy that hath no end.
("The Day of Resurrection," John of Damascus, trans.
John Mason Neale, *United Methodist Hymnal*, 303)

These are three of the greatest gifts of Easter, gifts that are so helpful to remember when the world takes the wind out of our sails—comfort when our hearts are heavy, the commission to continue Christ's ministry, and his companionship, which we can always claim and count on.

CHAPTER SEVEN

Remember That the Holy Spirit Is with You

SCRIPTURE: ROMANS 12:1-2; ACTS 2:1-4

Some years ago, there was a beauty pageant at the local rest home. One contestant entered the pageant who was one hundred years old at the time. Isn't that something? A hundred-year-old beauty pageant contestant!

She went out with the help of her family and got a manicure, a facial, a new dress, and had her hair styled. She looked really nice—but she lost.

But I like what she did. When she heard them call out somebody else's name as the winner, she marched right over to the judges' table, put her hands on her hips, and said to the judges, "I want to ask you a question. Did you see me?"

Way to go! I like that. She was saying to them, "Let's

go back and re-run this thing. You judges had better take another look!" And she probably walked away thinking, "Just you wait till next year!"

This hundred-year-old beauty pageant contestant knew she was a winner. She knew she looked good, and she was certain that those judges needed a little help with their vision. They needed their eyes fixed!

Don't we all? Don't we all need our eyes fixed so we can see better? Sometimes we just don't see things as clearly as we should, and we need a little help with our vision.

Well, that is precisely what Pentecost is all about. The Holy Spirit comes to inspire us and comfort us and guide us, and to clear up our vision. The disciples were waiting there in Jerusalem, not really sure what they were supposed to do next. They were confused and fuzzy. Their vision was clouded and uncertain. They wanted and needed help. They wanted the Holy Spirit to come and open their eyes, and that is exactly what happened. Remember the story with me.

Christ has been crucified. He has risen and appeared to the disciples. He has told them that he must leave them but that he will not leave them alone. He will send a comforter, a counselor. The Holy Spirit will come and be with them and give them power and courage and vision, and they will take up Christ's ministry and be his witnesses to all the world.

Jesus has ascended into heaven, and the disciples have returned to the Holy City to wait for the Holy Spirit. Now, here they are waiting and wondering, not sure how all of this is going to turn out, not sure just what they are supposed to do next.

They don't fully understand all that has happened. They don't see clearly what their task is yet. They sit there waiting—waiting and wondering. Then suddenly on the day of Pentecost they hear a sound—the rush of a mighty wind—the breath of God is blowing on that place. Immediately, they are all filled with the Holy Spirit, and they begin to speak out in other tongues. Now, don't mistake this for the unknown tongues. They are speaking in the languages of people of all the nations.

People hear the sounds and come running. A great crowd (thousands of people) assembles there, representing all the nations of the world—Asians, Arabians, Egyptians, Italians, Parthians, Medes, and Elamites.

Folks from everywhere, all nations and countries, gather, and they are amazed because each one of them hears his own native tongue being spoken. Someone in the crowd, bowled over by this communications miracle, cries out "What can this mean?"

But then some cynic answers (there's one in every crowd). The cynic says, "Aw, they're just drunk!"

Now this is the moment Simon Peter has been waiting for. He sees it all clearly now. The Holy Spirit has opened his eyes to see that Christ was not just a Jewish Messiah, but more the Savior of the world, the Lord of all people and all nations. Peter sees it now, and now he knows what he is supposed to do.

Simon Peter stands up and he begins to speak: "No! These men are not drunk. The Spirit of God is upon them and they realize now the truth of God as never before. Jesus of Nazareth, the one you crucified: God has raised him up! He has appeared to us. He is the Son of God, the Lord of life, the Savior of the whole world."

When the crowd heard that, they were ashamed of what they had done. They were cut to the heart: "You mean we tried to kill the Son of God! Oh no! What should we do?"

Peter answers, "It's not too late. God, in His grace, will forgive you. Repent and be baptized in the name of Jesus Christ for the forgiveness of your sins, and you too will receive this gift of the Holy Spirit. The promise is open to all. Whosoever will, may come. And the Scriptures tell us that three thousand souls were saved that day,.

The powerful story of Pentecost has much to teach us. The point is clear. Through the gift of the Holy Spirit, our hearts are warmed, our spirits are strengthened, and our eyes are opened. The coming of the Holy Spirit into our lives gives us new vision, a new way of looking at things.

Those disciples that Pentecost morning were not drunk. They were not filled with new wine. They were filled with the Spirit of God, and that Holy Spirit opened their eyes to incredible new possibilities. Let me show you what I mean.

First, Pentecost Gives Us a New Way of Looking at the World

Pentecost shows us dramatically that Christ is more than a Jewish Messiah. He is the Lord of life, the Christ for all people and all nations, the Savior of the world.

At Pentecost, the people were brought together in peace, harmony, and understanding. They could communicate. The Holy Spirit united them.

A number of years ago, Marshall McLuhan said that the advances in mass media, electronic communications, and travel have made our world a global village. Technological advances are shrinking the world more and more each day, and we have become not a big wide world anymore but a global village. This means that we must stop thinking of other nations as enemies and begin to see them as neighbors, members together of the world village.

Marshall McLuhan was right of course, but with all due respect to him, the global village concept was not really so new after all. Jesus taught us that a long time ago. In fact, he went even further. He said we are more than neighbors. We are brothers and sisters. We are family. We see that point demonstrated at Pentecost as the Holy Spirit brings together all those nations, and as Simon Peter tells them that we are brothers and sisters in Christ, and that whosoever will may come and be part of this family.

The Holy Spirit of God reminds us that:

> Jesus loves the little children,
> All the children of the world.
> Red and yellow, black and white,
> They are precious in His sight.
> Jesus loves the little children of the world.
> ("Jesus Loves the Little Children," lyrics by Clare Herbert Woolston, 1910)

The Holy Spirit opens our eyes. Pentecost gives us the eyes of love and inclusiveness; Pentecost gives us a new way of looking at the world.

Second, Pentecost Gives Us a New Way of Looking at Ourselves

At Pentecost, when Simon Peter laid it on the line and exposed people's sin, the Scriptures say graphically,

"They were cut to the heart" (Acts 2:37). Now, let me ask you something. Have you ever been cut to the heart?

They were ashamed and penitent. But look! Peter follows with words of grace: you can repent and you can be forgiven. God knows all about you and he still loves you.

Even though we sin, even though we fail, God still loves us and claims us. That's what the Holy Spirit comes to teach us.

I once heard a story about a priest who entered the priesthood after pursuing several colorful careers. This priest had been a soldier in Vietnam, a singer with a group that never quite took off, and a professional athlete. In his mid-thirties, he decided to go to seminary and train to be a priest. When he graduated, he was assigned to a parish in one of the toughest neighborhoods in New York City.

One day he got into an argument with a cab driver parked in front of the church. One word led to another, and suddenly the priest forgot the thin veneer of his new profession—so he grabbed the cabbie and pinned him up against a fence. The cabbie seemed to be reaching for a knife, but fortunately other people stepped in and broke it up before anyone got hurt.

The priest was mortified at what he had done and

how he had acted. He knew that this was no way for a man of the cloth to deal with conflict. He was so ashamed, cut to the heart. He later described the feeling: "It was terrible. A few minutes later I had to say Mass with that ugliness, that hate, that anger rising in me. It hurt to pray. I was confused. What does 'love your neighbor' mean? I looked up at the cross, and I knew I had failed. I had not loved my enemy. I had wanted to fight."

He wondered if he was worthy to be a priest. While he was grappling with his soul, the priest had a visitor, a little girl who came by the church every morning to get a glass of milk, because the church is located in a poor neighborhood. This little girl knew nothing of what had happened, but she gave her priest something that morning that brought him out of his spiritual crisis. It was a note scribbled out with a first-grade pencil. It read: "I love you once. I love you twice. I love you more than beans and rice."

That's all, but it was just what the priest needed. He said, "I read her poem and I smiled. . . . I understood the larger message, too. [She] had reminded me what's really important. To me she was an angel [a messenger from God]. [She] reminded me that we are loved and accepted as we are. God sends us messengers like that, but sometimes we miss them."

This is the message of Pentecost. Even though we sin, even though we fail, God still loves us and claims us and redeems us. The Holy Spirit comes to teach us that Pentecost gives us the word of grace and forgiveness and enables us to look at ourselves in a new way.

Finally, Pentecost Gives Us a New Way of Looking at Christ

"Pistol" Pete Maravich was without question one of the greatest basketball players who ever lived. Many of his basketball records still stand. But Pete Maravich had an unsettled and empty life until he met Jesus Christ. Here's how he described it shortly before he died:.

> I told God and everyone else, "I don't need you. I'm going to play basketball, get a world championship ring and make a million dollars." The basketball court and the arena were my refuge. But when I left them and retired from playing, I could not face present reality. I kept trying to live in the past . . . and I used alcohol and other escapes to do so. Although I was miserable, I still fancied myself the college star I once was, basking in my former glory. Then in 1982 . . . I accepted Jesus Christ, whom I had kept safely between the pages of the Sunday school leaflets I had received as a child.
>
> Giving my life to Christ has changed me dramatically. I wouldn't trade my life in Him for 1,000 NBA championships, 1,000 Hall of Fame rings, or one hundred billion dollars.

(Pete Maravich and Darrel Campbell, *Heir to a Dream* [Nashville: Thomas Nelson, 1987])

That's what Pentecost teaches us. That's what the Holy Spirit teaches us—that life in Christ is the most valuable and the most important thing in all the world.

CHAPTER EIGHT

Remember That the Spiritual Disciplines Do Work

SCRIPTURE: ACTS 2:43-47

A few years ago I received a newsletter from Dr. Leonard Sweet. At the time, Dr. Sweet was the dean of the seminary at Drew University. In his letter he was reflecting on some of the alarming changes that are happening in our world today.

To document his concern, Dr. Sweet shared some statistics from the California Department of Education, which compare the top seven discipline problems in public schools in the 1940s with the top twelve discipline problems in public schools today. Indeed, how times have changed.

In the 1940s the top seven discipline problems were

1. Talking in class

2. Chewing gum
3. Making noise
4. Running in the halls
5. Getting out of turn in line
6. Wearing improper clothing
7. Not putting paper in waste baskets

Now, put that over against this. Today the top twelve discipline problems in our public schools are

1. Drug and alcohol abuse
2. Pregnancy
3. Suicide
4. Rape
5. Robbery, assault with deadly weapons, and burglary
6. Arson or bombings
7. Murder
8. Absenteeism
9. Vandalism
10. Gang warfare
11. Abortion
12. Venereal disease

Each one of these twelve problems tells its own horror story. For example, take No. 2, pregnancy. In the year 1991, there were 150,000 live births where the mothers of these new babies were between the ages of nine and fourteen. This does not include abortions and miscarriages. There were 150,000 babies born in one year to children aged nine through fourteen. Do I have your attention? Disturbing statistics like these do raise a number of serious questions:

- Where are we heading?
- What will a similar list in this decade look like?
- What would a list of "adult discipline problems today" include?
- How do we prepare our children and ourselves to face these difficult and frightening problems?
- Why are things changing so dramatically?

The folk singer was right: "The Times They Are a-Changin'." It's important for us to recognize that, but I think it's even more essential for us to recognize that

- there are some things in this life that never change.
- there are some things in this life that we can always count on.
- there are some things in this life that are pure and eternal, constant and solid and unshakable.
- there are some fixed points in this ever-changing world.

- there are some dependable spiritual laws woven into the fabric of life that never change, that fit every age, every generation, and every situation.

We see thses spiritual constants in the Ten Commandments. We see them in the life and teachings of Jesus. We see them in the letters of the apostle Paul. We see them in the actions of those early Christians in the first century.

Anyone awake enough to "smell the coffee" can easily see that

- life is better when we love God and we love other people.
- life is better when we honor our parents and respect one another and tell the truth.
- life is better when we are honest and faithful, and kind and gracious in all our relationships.
- life is better when we live daily by the disciplines of discipleship.

But what are these disciplines of discipleship? There are many, of course, but in our scripture lesson for today, we discover three significant holy habits from those early Christians—three prevailing themes that flow out of this scripture passage at the end of Acts 2.

At Pentecost, the Holy Spirit came upon the disciples dramatically, and look at what they did—they worshiped together; they trusted God's teachings; and they loved and helped one another.

If we would concentrate on those three things, if we would really give our hearts and souls to them, then we, like the early disciples, could stand tall in any story. Indeed, with the help of God, we could turn the world upside down. Look with me now at these three significant disciplines of discipleship that never change.

First of All, There Is the Discipline of Worship

When the world takes the wind out of our sails, some of us make the mistake of saying: "I'm in a hard valley right now. Let me get my act together and then I will come back to church." But you see, this kind of thinking misses the point. It is worship and the support of the church family that help us get our act together. It is the church that helps us find God's healing, redeeming, saving power. But it's true, isn't it? Going to church is indeed a discipline! It's a commitment! It's a holy habit! And I think it is much more important than most people realize, maybe even more important today than ever before because of the frantic pace of our lives these days. We are always on the run, constantly on the go.

Virginia Brasier put it well when she wrote these lines:

This is the age of the half-read page,
The quick hash and the mad dash.

Now, where in this frenzied, hectic pace of life is there time for God? Time for centering down and focusing in on God and his will for our lives? Where is the time for meditation and prayer and spiritual reflections and remembering the priorities? The words of Leslie Weatherhead are helpful here. He said, "If faith matters...and to my mind it matters as food and fresh air matter...then we must make time for God." We must discipline ourselves to make time for God.

A group of nine- and ten-year-olds attended worship service one Sunday morning and then each wrote a letter to the minister reflecting on the experience. Here are some of the better ones:

- *Dear Reverend, I liked your sermon Sunday, especially when it was finished.* Ralph, age 10.

- *Dear Reverend, My father likes to sit in the last row in the church so he can sneak out during the sermon. Sometimes my mother stops him before he sneaks out...but not last Sunday.* Denise, age 10.

- Margaret, age 10, wrote: *Dear Reverend, I like to go to church every Sunday because I don't have any choice.*

- Justin, age 9, wrote: *Dear Reverend, Thank you for your sermon Sunday. I will write more when my mother explains to me what you said.*

- Loreen, age 9, wrote her letter with an interesting suggestion: *Dear Reverend, I think more people would come to church if you would move it to Disneyland.*

- Here is the one that caught my attention. This came from Marcia, age 10: *Dear Reverend, My grandparents go to church more than anyone else in the family. I think it's because they have known God longer.*

There's a lot of truth to that last letter. Those who are attentive to spiritual matters, who have spent time with God, do indeed have a growing knowledge of God and a growing love for him. Many years ago, the famous Christian mystic Meister Eckhart said it like this: "God does not work in all hearts alike, but according to the preparation and sensitivity He finds in each." What that means is, you can't hear the music of God unless you are tuned in! The discipline of worship is important.

Some years ago a speedboat driver was racing at top speed when his boat suddenly veered slightly and hit a wave at a dangerous angle. The combination of his speed and the size and angle of the wave sent the boat spinning crazily into the air. The driver was thrown from his seat and propelled into the water. He was pushed so deep into the water that he had no idea which direction the surface was. For a moment he went into a panic, flailing wildly at the water, but then he came to his senses. He stopped flailing, he got still and quiet, and he waited. He let his life vest work for him. He let his life vest begin to pull him up. Once he discovered which way was up, he then swam quickly to the surface and was saved.

Worship is that time in the week when we stop flailing at life, when we wait quietly, and when we rediscover which way is up! That's the first thing. It's so crucial—the discipline of worship.

Second, There Is the Discipline of Trust

Once, there was a shepherd boy named Hans. He had been trained well by his father, but like most teenagers, sometimes he would let his mind wander, sometimes he didn't pay attention as closely as he should have. Late one winter afternoon, Hans was bringing the sheep home from the mountain when suddenly, without warning, a ferocious snowstorm hit. Hans wanted to turn and take the sheep away from the storm, but he vaguely remembered something his dad had told him some years before. "Hans, if you are ever caught in a snowstorm, don't retreat! Go right into the face of the storm."

Everything within Hans resisted that advice. More than anything, he wanted to take the sheep away from the storm. But he knew how wise his father was, and he trusted his father's teaching. He knew his father had explained the reason for heading into the storm, but for the life of him Hans couldn't remember the details. He couldn't remember the explanation. But Hans knew that he could count on his father's words, and so even though it didn't seem logical to him at the moment, and even though everything within him resisted it, Hans decided to trust his father's counsel. He drove the sheep forward right into the face of the storm. The sheep didn't want to go that way, but Hans and his dog pushed them forward. It was tough. It was difficult. The wind and snow blew hard against them, and Hans could hardly see. It was painful and frightening, but he kept driving the flock into the face of the storm. Finally, as they came out of the worst of it, Hans could see his father and his brothers coming to meet him and help him, and they were able to get all the sheep safely home.

"We were worried about you," his father said. Hans answered, "Father, I did just what you told me to do. I kept going into the face of the storm, but I have to tell you I couldn't remember why you told me to do it that way. I wanted so much to go the other way. I wanted so much to run away from the storm."

"If you had," his father said, "it would have been disastrous. The wind would have blown the fur of the sheep upward and the snow would have gotten in and formed ice, and the sheep would have frozen to death. Hans, you did the right thing, and I am so proud of you."

That's a parable for us, isn't it? It's about the discipline of trust, the discipline of trusting our Father's teaching in every circumstance—even when we don't want to do it, even when we don't understand all the ins and outs of it. If we will discipline ourselves to trust God and his instructions in every situation, he will bring us through the storm; he will bring us safely home.

First, there is the discipline of worship; and second, there is the discipline of trust.

Third and Finally, There Is the Discipline of Love

Jesus did not give many commandments, but on that dramatic night in the Upper Room he gave a new commandment to his disciples and to all who would follow after them. He said, "I give you a new commandment, that you love one another. Just as I have loved you . . ." (John 13:34).

Recently my brother shared with me a beautiful story about a woman who became seriously ill and spent the last few months of her life confined to her bed. A mockingbird would come regularly and sing just outside of her window. One day she began whistling, just to see if she could get the mockingbird to imitate her whistle. Amazingly, the mockingbird rose to the occasion. She would whistle, and the mockingbird would repeat the sound precisely. Whatever this lady would whistle, the mockingbird would mock that. One day shortly before she died, she began to whistle that famous beginning of Beethoven's Fifth Symphony, and the mockingbird quickly responded, repeating the melody perfectly. In the days ahead, she became weaker and could whistle no more. But every day without fail, the mockingbird would come to her window and serenade her with Beethoven.

At her funeral, the minister told the story about her teaching the mockingbird to whistle, and he concluded by saying, "Somewhere in the world, there is a mockingbird that sings Beethoven because of her."

Now, let me ask you something. Is there someone somewhere in this world today who sings Christ's song of love because of you? That's our calling—to pass on to others the discipline of worship, the discipline of trust, and the discipline of love.

CHAPTER NINE

Remember That There Is Help Available

SCRIPTURE: NUMBERS 11:13-17

A few years ago I was asked to lead a workshop at a national convention for schoolteachers. The topic they assigned me was an interesting one: "How to Cope with Stress Creatively!" When I arrived at the convention center, I was told to go to the main lobby and check in with the registrar. Now, the registrar was a large, powerful, take-charge woman who looked and acted very much like a person who would be equally at home as a professional wrestler or as a drill sergeant for a U. S. Marines boot camp. She was barking out orders authoritatively, and her assistants were jumping to obey her commands. Finally, she turned her attention to me. "You," she said, "step over here!"

I said what anyone in his right mind would have said

in that moment—"Yes ma'am"—and I stepped over in front of her.

When I told her my name, immediately she said, "I've been looking for you. You're going to have the biggest group. We have sixty-three different workshops for the teachers to choose from, but you will have twice as many in your group as any of the rest." Before I even had a chance to swell with pride, she quickly added, "Now, don't go getting the big head, because the big attendance has nothing to do with you!"

"Oh?" I said quizzically.

"No," she said, "It's not you. It's your subject! If we want to get the teachers out for a workshop, all we have to do is use either the word *stress* or the word *cope*, and you've got both of them in your title: 'How to Cope with Stress Creatively!' The teachers will come running to that, because they feel stressed to the max these days, and they need all the help they can get."

She was right. I did have a large group, and it quickly became dramatically obvious that they were indeed feeling great stress on the job. And the teachers are not alone. Many people are feeling stress in their professions today—including ministers.

Recently I ran across two different surveys that listed the top ten most stressful jobs in the world today. In the first survey, the ministry was listed as the seventh most stressful job. In the second survey, the ministry was not listed at all. I assumed there must be some mistake, so I looked under clergy. It wasn't there either. I looked under "pastor," "preacher," "priest." Not there. I felt a little disappointed. Strangely, I liked the first survey best. I liked the one that listed the ministry as the number seven most stressful job, probably for a couple of reasons.

For one thing, I didn't want to think that all that worrying I've been doing for the last thirty years was for nothing. Also, have you ever noticed that most of us sort of like to think that our job is stressful? We don't want other people to think we have an easy time of it.

Some time ago I saw a cartoon that underscores this point. It depicts a big office, a huge desk, a CEO type sitting behind the desk. In front of the desk, there's a little man in work clothes, his hat in his hands, and he is saying to the CEO, "If it's any comfort, sir, it's lonely at the bottom too!"

No question about it—these are stressful times. All of us at times feel stretched to the breaking point. We all sometimes feel pulled apart at the seams. We all know what it feels like to be stressed to the max.

Some writers these days would have us believe that stress is a modern-day problem caused by the hectic, pressure-packed world in which we live. Yet, though we would be quick to agree that there are indeed some new stress factors today caused by the frantic pace and hard demands of our contemporary, competitive world, it is also true that stress is as old as the Bible.

Did you know that, of all people, Moses had stress on the job? That is precisely what this passage in Numbers 11 is all about. Moses had had it. He was trying his best to lead the people out of Egyptian slavery to the promised land, and he was fed up with the problems and complaints. He was suffering from burnout. The red flags were obvious. He was feeling overworked and underappreciated. He was tired of the pressures, the demands, the responsibilities, and the burdens of leadership. And he was bone-weary with all the griping and groaning and criticizing. Everything was going wrong.

Their problems fell neatly into three categories. For one thing, they were having a hard time reaching their destination. It took them forty years to travel from Egypt to the promised land, a distance of only about two hundred miles, like from Houston to San Antonio. So short a way to go, so long a time to get there. Moses' wife said it took forty years because Moses would never stop and ask for directions.

And second, they ran out of food. So God had to give them something called manna to eat. Nobody knows for sure what manna was. Garrison Keillor says *manna* is Hebrew for "tuna casserole."

Then third, the people began to complain. "Why did you do this to us, Moses? We were better off as slaves in Egypt. Why didn't you just leave us alone?" Finally, Moses, stressed out, turns to God for help. This brings us to our Scripture in Numbers 11:

> So the LORD said to Moses: "Gather for me seventy of the elders of Israel, whom you know to be the elders of the people and officers over them; bring them to the tent of meeting, and have them take their place there with you. I will come down and talk with you there; and I will take some of the spirit that is on you and put it on them; and they shall bear the burden of the people along with you so that you will not bear it all by your-self." (Numbers 11:16-17)

What an amazing passage this is! Even though it was written thousands of years ago, its message is as fresh as the morning sun. Look at the practical advice here. Stress is the result of carrying too much weight in your life. Ask any engineer. Ask any doctor. They will tell you about that. You put too much stress on one part, and you will soon see stress fractures. So let's take this practical advice from the Old Testament and apply it to our lives today. This text in Numbers 11 gives us a simple yet profound three-point formula to use when we feel completely stressed out. Let me show you how it works.

First of All, When You Feel Stressed Out, Let Your Friends Help You

Delegate some of the burden to other people. That is exactly what God told Moses to do. Don't try to carry it all yourself. Share the load with others. Let your friends help you. That's what friends are for.

Some years ago, a group of American theologians traveled to Africa to visit Albert Schweitzer at his jungle hospital on the Ogowe River. The theologians spent three days with Dr. Schweitzer and were greatly moved by the experience and by the unique privilege of spending time with this giant of a man.

One event, however, stood out in a special way. It was close to noon and extremely hot. The group was walking up a steep hill with Dr. Schweitzer. Albert Schweitzer was eighty-five years old at the time. Suddenly, Dr. Schweitzer said, "Please excuse me." He broke away from the group and ran across the slope of the hill to a place where an African woman was struggling with a huge armload of wood for the cook fires. The American theologians watched with admiration and concern as the eighty-five-year-old Albert Schweitzer helped the woman carry that heavy load on up the hill.

When they all reached the top of the hill, one of the Americans asked Dr. Schweitzer why he did things like that, implying that in that extreme heat and at his age he shouldn't do such things. Albert Schweitzer only smiled and then, pointing to the woman, said simply: "No one should ever have to carry a burden like that alone."

That's what God was saying to Moses back there during the Exodus: *This is too big a load for any one person to carry. It's too stressful to try to do this all by yourself. Let your friends help you.* That's number one: when you feel stressed to the max, delegate some of the burden to other people. Let your friends help you.

Second, When You Feel Stressed Out, Let Your Church Help You

When Moses was about ready to throw in the towel, look what God said to him: "Go to the tent of meeting. Go to the church." Some folks go about it all wrong. They get under stress, and they stay away from the church. "Let me get my act together, and then I'll get back in church," they say. But that's not the way it works. It's the church that can help us get our act together.

I once saw a young man get stressed to the max at a wedding. Unfortunately, he happened to be the groom. The night before, at the rehearsal, it was the bride who seemed so nervous, but the groom was something else. He was calm, cool, macho, and laid back—at the rehearsal. However, on the day of the wedding there was a role reversal: the bride was perfectly serene and calm, and the groom was a wreck! I was giving him his vows and noticed that he was turning whiter and whiter. I stopped and whispered, "Are you OK?"

He answered, "I think I'll be all right, Dr. Smith." I knew right then we were in serious trouble. I continued with his vows, and suddenly I saw in this young man a part of the human eyeball I had never seen before as his eyes rolled somewhere in the back of his head.

Suddenly, he bolted and ran out the side door. The bride looked at me as calm as she could be and said, "Jim, what do we do now?"

I said, "I don't have a clue, but wait here and let me go check on him." I told the congregation to hold their places, the groom was a little under the weather, and we would be back in just a moment.

When I reached the groom outside, he said, "I'm okay now. I thought I was going to pass out, and I had to get out of there." Then he said, "I can't go back in there. I'm too embarrassed. There's no way I'm going back in there to be laughed at."

I said, "Well, before we make that decision, let me ask you two questions. First, do you love her?"

"Oh, yes," he said.

"Second, do you want to be married to her?"

"Oh, yes! She's the best thing that's ever happened to me."

Then I said, "Well, let's go back and finish this ceremony. The church will not laugh at you. They will welcome you back with open arms. They will support you in every way."

When we stepped back into the sanctuary, the most amazing happened. With no coaching from anybody, everyone in the church began to applaud. The groom smiled, and then, like a Shakespearean actor, he took a deep bow! It was just the right touch: the church gave him a standing ovation! It gave him confidence, strength, and assurance. He came back to the altar. His bride hugged him and kissed him, and then we proceeded with the ceremony. That was many years ago, and today they are still happily married.

That's an interesting parable to me because it speaks volumes about how the church can help and heal and strengthen and reassure.

In his letter to the church at Galatia, the apostle Paul put it like this: "Bear one another's burdens, and so fulfill the law of Christ" (6:2). When you feel "stressed to the max," let your friends help you, and let your church help you.

Third and Finally, When You Feel Completely Stressed Out, Let Your God Help You

The comedian Richard Pryor spent the early years of his professional career trying to get ahead, trying to make money, trying to be a success. But then one day he was critically burned. For days and days in the hospital he fought for his life. The doctors didn't know if he would make it or not. His life hung in the balance between life and death for some time. Finally, he did pull through, he did survive, and he did recover. Shortly after being released from the hospital, he made his first public appearance since the accident, on *The Tonight Show* with Johnny Carson. Richard Pryor told Johnny Carson that when you are critically ill like that, money is suddenly not important anymore. He said, "All I could think of was to call on God." He said, "I didn't call the Bank of America a single time. All I could do was call on God."

This is the most crucial thing to remember about this amazing passage in Numbers 11. Moses felt "stressed to the max," and he called out to God, and God was there! God heard his cry, and God helped him. When you feel totally stressed out, when the world takes the wind out of your sails, don't try to carry that burden all by yourself. Let your friends help you, let your church help you, and most important of all, let your God help you.

CHAPTER TEN

Remember to Pray in the Spirit of Christ

SCRIPTURE: JOHN 14:12-14

When the world takes the wind out of your sails, it's important to remember to pray, and it is crucial to remember to pray in the spirit of Christ. Let me share with you some quotes about prayer that I find fascinating.

First, George Buttrick, in his significant book entitled *Prayer*, says this: "Prayer is either the primary fact of the religious life or it is the world's worst delusion."

Next, Gaston Foote, who was for many years pastor of First Methodist Church in Fort Worth, once said: "The heart of the Christian religion is the prayer life. The more we seek fellowship with God through prayer, the more Godlike we become. The great saints, without exception, have been persons who spent hours and hours in prayer."

Then, too, Dr. Alexis Carrel, who was a physician, scientist, author, and Nobel Prize winner, wrote these words:

> Prayer is...the most powerful form of energy that we can generate....Its results mean increased buoyancy, greater intellectual vigor, moral stamina, and a deeper understanding of human relationships. Prayer is indispensable to the fullest development of personality. Only in prayer do we achieve that complete harmonious assembly of mind, body and spirit which gives the frail human reed its unshakeable strength.

Now, these are all powerful and eloquent statements about prayer. Yet, let's be honest and admit that despite these wonderful-sounding accolades about prayer many, many people are frustrated in their prayer lives. Many people get discouraged, and they drop out on their faith because they feel that they fail in their prayer lives or that their prayers have failed them. They feel that they are not "getting through," so they give it all up.

A classic illustration of this is found in Mark Twain's book *The Adventures of Huckleberry Finn*. Remember Huck Finn's account of prayer and how he quit praying because it did not produce the results he wanted? Listen again to his words:

> Miss Watson she took me in the closet and prayed, but nothing come of it. She told me to pray every day, and whatever I asked for I would get it. But it warn't so. I

tried it. Once I got a fish-line, but no hooks. It warn't any good to me without hooks. I tried for the hooks three or four times, but somehow I couldn't make it work. By and by, one day, I asked Miss Watson to try for me, but she said I was a fool. She never told me why, and I couldn't make it out no way.... I says to myself, if a body can get anything they pray for, why don't Deacon Winn get back the money he lost on pork? Why can't the widow get back her silver snuff-box that was stole? Why can't Miss Watson fat up? No, says I to myself, there ain't nothing in it!

Of course, Huck Finn's approach to prayer was naive and simplistic and selfish. It was a complete distortion and misunderstanding of prayer, and it was doomed from the start. However, we can find ourselves identifying with Huckleberry Finn in his dilemma, because we have been told over and over again that prayer works miracles, that through prayer all things are possible if only we believe.

Such statements like these do have the ring of truth in them, but they cannot be pressed to the absurd. God does indeed have many wonderful things to give us, but please do not picture God as some kind of celestial waiter who takes our order and then swiftly returns with steaming plates of whatever we ask for. God is not our servant. He is our sovereign Lord. Jesus did not say, "Whatever you ask for you shall receive." He didn't say that. He did say,

"Whatever you ask for in My Name you shall receive" (John 14:13, author's paraphrase). Underscore those three words *in My Name*. And to understand more clearly what this means, just scratch out the word *name* and put in its place the word *Spirit*. Jesus says, "Whatever you ask for in My Spirit you shall receive." This is the key to a meaningful prayer life, praying in the spirit of Christ. That is, only when our prayers are loving and humble and obedient to God's will, only then do they become powerful, effective Christian prayers.

You see, I can't pray that I'll win twenty million dollars and be in the spirit of Christ. I can't pray that I'll inherit a new Mercedes and be in the spirit of Christ. I can't pray that I'll beat you in an election and be in the spirit of Christ. Praying "in the name of Christ" is not just a nice phrase we tack onto the end of our prayers as a kind of letter of endorsement. No! It means coming to God in the loving spirit of Christ. It means praying as Christ would pray. It means praying in a Christlike way. Let me show you what I mean with a few quick thoughts.

First, It's OK to Ask God to Bless Us, but It Is Not Christlike to Ask God to Bless Us at the Expense of Others

We can't ask God to bless us at the expense of others and be in the spirit of Christ. Let me illustrate. Some years ago at a youth camp, I heard a young high school girl give a testimony on how God answered her prayer. She said more than anything she wanted to be a cheerleader. She prayed and prayed about it, begging God to let her win a spot on the squad. When the results were posted, she didn't quite make it, but she made first alternate. She said at the first practice one of the other girls fell and broke her leg. Then she said, "I was elevated to cheerleader, and that's how God answered my prayer."

I cringed inside. Can we believe that God would break the leg of one of his children in order to answer the prayer of another of his children? How warped can we be in our thinking to imagine that God would inflict pain on somebody else in order to bless us? I can't pray that God would bless *me* at your expense. I can't do that and be in the spirit of Christ. Have you heard about the woman who planned a garden party, but then the day before the party as she looked back over the guest list, she was shocked to realize that she had failed to invite her best friend, who was her next-door neighbor? Hurriedly, she called, explained, and pleaded with her next-door neighbor to come to the garden party. "It's too late," mourned the neighbor. "I've already prayed for rain!"

It's unfair to ask God to bless us at the expense of others. Here is a second unfair prayer.

Second, It's OK to Ask God to Forgive Us, but It's Not Christlike to Expect Him to Sweep Away Instantaneously the Consequences of Our Wrongdoings

Let me stress that again: it's all right to ask for God's forgiveness. He wants to forgive us. Forgiveness is at hand. All we have to do is accept it. But it's not Christlike to expect God to wipe away or sweep away the consequences of our wrongdoing. If I erupt in a fit of temper and break your arm, God will forgive me if I am genuinely penitent, but your arm will still be broken, and we both have to live with that. If I steal money out of your cash register, God will forgive me if I am genuinely penitent, but he will not repay the money; I have to do that. If I start a cruel and malicious rumor about you, God will forgive me if I am genuinely penitent, but we still have to live with the pain and the agonizing consequences of hateful gossip, which is so hard to stop once we start it.

Remember Zacchaeus in the Gospel of Luke. Christ came into his life bringing forgiveness, but Zacchaeus came down out of that sycamore tree trying his best to do his part to redeem his past. "Half of my possessioins, Lord, I will give to the poor; and if I have defrauded anyone of anything, I will pay back four times as much" (Luke 19:8). Zacchaeus faced the consequences of what he had done and what he had become, and he was trying to correct it, trying to make it right. We have to do that too. God will forgive us, but we cannot expect him to instantaneously sweep away the consequences of our wrongdoings.

Third, It's OK to Pray for Others Lovingly, but It's Not Christlike to Pray for Others Critically

You can't pray critically or harshly about others and be in the spirit of Christ. Listen closely now: what we know today as the most offensive kind of profanity (the taking of the Lord's name in vain) began as ancient people prayed hatefully to their gods, urging them to put curses on other people. I won't say those words in this book. I won't say them anywhere; I don't like to hear them. But those terrible words, the taking of the Lord's name in vain, were (originally) horribly misguided prayers, vindictive, critical, cruel prayers beseeching God to lay a curse on another person, urging God to destroy someone's soul.

We pray critically in another way too, and it sounds so pious. Remember the Pharisee in the temple praying, "God, I thank you that I am not like other people: thieves, rogues, adulterers, or even like this tax collector" (Luke 18:11). Please beware of being "holier than thou" in your praying. Pray for others lovingly—not critically, not judgmentally.

Recently, a woman came in to see me. She was a drifter, a transient, and a real character: I realized that right away because she told me in a very hostile tone that she was the Holy Spirit and that she had forgotten more about the Bible and religion than I would ever know. Then she proceeded to tell me that she had just come from Birmingham, Alabama, where she had prayed and prayed for a minister there and got him converted, and that now she had come to pray for me. I was not sure that I wanted her to pray for me in the way she had in mind!

The point is this: it's good to pray for others lovingly, tenderly, graciously, and mercifully but never critically. We can't do that and be in the spirit of Christ.

Fourth, It's OK to Ask God to Help Us, but It's Not Christlike to Expect God to Do for Us What We Can Easily Do for Ourselves

It is not Christlike to expect God to cover for us when we haven't done our part. This was Huckleberry Finn's problem, wasn't it? He was praying for fishing hooks when he could have easily gotten fishing hooks for himself. William Barclay once reminded us that "prayer is not a labor saving device." How many times have students walked into classrooms praying frantically, "Lord, I didn't study, but if you will just slip me the answers this time, I'll do better next time"? But you see, God expects us to do the best we can with what we have, and then he will be with us in it.

Let me share with you one of my favorite stories. I used it in one of the first sermons I preached. It's about a little boy who went fishing with his father. They put out a "trotline" and went in for lunch. As they came back to check the line, the little boy said, "Daddy, I bet we caught a lot of fish." Sure enough, as they pulled up the line, there was a fish on almost every hook.

"How did you know?" asked the father.

The little boy said, "I prayed about it."

This same thing happened twice more that afternoon. The little boy would predict confidently that there would be lots of fish on the line, and when it turned out that way, he would say, "I prayed about it." But as they came out to fish the next morning, the boy said, "Dad, we are not going to have a single fish on the line." And he was right. As they pulled up the line, they saw that they had not caught a fish.

"Didn't you pray?" asked the father.

"No," answered the son.

"Why not?" asked the father.

And the little boy answered, "Because we forgot to bait the hooks."

That's precisely the point: it's not enough just to pray.

We have to do our part. We have to pray and work. We have to bait the hooks. We can't expect God to do it all for us.

Finally, It's Not Christlike to Ask God for Anything That Is Inconsistent with His Will and Purpose

If you want to pray in the spirit of Christ, then pray, "Thy will be done." That is the best, most Christlike prayer of all. As I prepared this chapter, I went back and looked again at the great prayers of the saints. Do you know what I discovered? I found that rarely, if ever, did they ask God for anything except the closer knowledge of his will and the strength to follow it. The great people of faith were more concerned with God's will than with their wants. They were more concerned with God's direction than with their desires. They were more concerned with God's purposes than with their possessions. The great men and women of faith seem to be content simply to be in God's presence, to reflect on the wonder and mystery of his Being, and to commit themselves afresh to be the earthen vessels of his will.

In a word, when you study the prayers of the spiritual giants, you discover that the great saints became as little children before God. Remember what they said about Dietrich Bonhoeffer: "He was a giant before men because he was a child before God." Isn't that beautiful?

Do you remember how Jesus prayed with childlike faith in the Garden of Gethsemane? With the cross looming before him, he prayed, "Abba, Father,... not what I want, but what you want" (Mark 14:36). Notice how Jesus addresses God here—"Abba." It was the word used in the home when a little child called his or her father. If we had an equivalent in English today, it would be *Daddy.* "Abba, Father," Jesus said, "Thy will be done."

Then, too, remember how on the cross Jesus prayed, "Father, into your hands I commend my spirit" (Luke 23:46). This was a prayer. And it was not the first time Jesus had prayed that prayer. This was the prayer Jewish mothers taught their children to pray when they went to bed at night. It was the bedtime prayer of little children in the time of Jesus. It was a quote from the Thirty-first Psalm: "Into your hand I commit my spirit" (v. 5).

Let me sum it all up now. Whatever we ask in the name of Jesus—that is, whatever we ask in the loving spirit of Christ—is appropriate and beautiful. Anything else is suspect. So, when the world tries to take the wind out of your sails it is important to pray, it is crucial to pray, but remember to pray in the spirit of Christ.

CHAPTER ELEVEN

Remember That You Can Spread Your Problems Before the Lord

SCRIPTURE: 2 KINGS 19:14

I recently saw the musical *Fiddler on the Roof* again. You may remember how it starts. A fiddler is standing precariously on a steep rooftop, playing his fiddle. The main character, Tevye, points to him and suggests that the fiddler symbolizes all the people of the village: they are all trying to maintain their balance, all trying to keep from slipping and falling. The winds blow against them; the footing is unsure; the situation is treacherous; the future is uncertain. But even as they face their problems, they try to make a little music along the way. Then as the story unfolds further, Tevye tries to make a little music and make a little sense out of it all as he faces over and over again bad news, impossible problems, and difficult people.

I guess the "fiddler on the roof" is a symbol for all of us, too. We can identify with him and relate to him because we all know full well from our own personal experience the dilemma of trying to deal with problems, keep our balance, and yet still make a little music along the way. I know this. All pastors share one common fact of life: we encounter persons daily who are trying to figure out how to handle bad news, impossible problems, and difficult people.

How is it with you? What are your circumstances? What hurt are you feeling? What anguish are you experiencing? What news is bad? What problems overwhelm you? Is there someone who is giving you a difficult time? What are your troubles, and how are you handling them?

Let me tell you a story that may help us here. It comes out of the Old Testament. It's the story of a king called Hezekiah. He lived some seven hundred years before Christ. He was the king of Judah. His father, Ahaz, was one of the worst kings, but Hezekiah became one of the most faithful kings to ever reign in Judah. He came to power in Jerusalem when he was twenty-five years old. He reigned for twenty-nine years. He was a great reformer. He destroyed the pagan idols and called the people back to the faith of Moses. He worshiped God and held fast to the commandments.

But life was not easy for Hezekiah. It seldom is for a great person of faith. The Assyrians were at the peak of their power. They had already conquered the northern kingdom, and now the Assyrian King Sennacherib was attacking the cities of Judah and capturing them. Sennacherib was vain and power-hungry, and he was moving toward Jerusalem.

King Hezekiah begged for understanding. Hezekiah gave Sennacherib all the treasury of the temple and all the treasury from the king's house. But it was not enough. Sennacherib and the Assyrians wanted more. Their lust for money and land and power was insatiable. Archaeologists have discovered the Taylor Cylinder in which Sennacherib bragged about capturing forty-six cities in Judah, taking over 200,000 human captives and huge numbers of cattle and animals of every kind. Hezekiah had paid literally millions of dollars worth of gold and silver. Still, Sennacherib wanted more. He sent word to the people of Jerusalem, telling them to surrender. "Don't listen to Hezekiah anymore. If you do, you are doomed. Hezekiah will tell you to trust God, but pay no attention to him. Your God is powerless against mighty Assyria. Hezekiah is powerless. Surrender now, and you will prosper."

Don't you see it? Hezekiah's world was crumbling. Here it was facing him—bad news, impossible problems, difficult people.

In our own ways, each of us has been there, haven't we? I talked to a man recently whose wife had been killed in an automobile accident. I asked how he was doing. He said, "My world has tumbled in." What do we do when our world tumbles in? How do we handle the downs of life? How do we handle bad news, impossible problems, and difficult people?

Over the years, several unsatisfactory answers have been given. For example, some say, tough it out on your own. Woody Hayes, the famous coach, told us, "When the going gets tough, the tough get going!" Sometimes that works, for a while that may work; but there are other times when our human resources are just not strong enough. We need a Savior beyond our own strength.

Some try to handle their problems in another way. They become bitter and cynical toward life. They become resentful and angry toward God. "How could God let this happen to me? What did I do to deserve this?" So they go on a "pity trip" and blame it on God.

And some turn after other gods. This is what Hezekiah's father had done. He turned to the Canaanite gods, and he built altars to Baal. He tried soothsaying and wizardry. Isn't it interesting how cultic religion has a weird fascination for people in trouble? Astrology, fortune-telling, "off-brand" religions—these cults find people who are troubled, vulnerable, easily taken in.

Still others give up when their world tumbles in. Throw in the towel, lower the flag: "I give up and give in."

I'm sure that Hezekiah was tempted toward all of the options. They can be persuasive when your back is against the wall. But Hezekiah stopped. He assessed the situation and he found a better option. By his pattern we can learn how to better handle bad news, impossible problems, and difficult people.

Look at what Hezekiah did. We see his response reflected here as the story continues to unfold. He was at the lowest point. He saw no way out. Not only were the Assyrians at the peak of their power, but now they have zeroed in on him. They have mocked him publicly, and now they threaten him. Knowing that he is a man of God, they sent him a letter, specifically warning him what will happen to him if he simply trusts his God. They reminded him of all the nations that they had already destroyed and told him he was next. King Hezekiah received the letter from the messengers and read it. Talk about bad news, impossible problems, and difficult people! Here we find all of that and more reflected in this frightening, threatening letter.

Now, look what Hezekiah did: He took the letter. He went up to the temple, and (I love this) he spread it before the Lord. That's how the Scriptures describe it:

"He spread it before the LORD." He spread the whole problem—letter and all—out before the Lord. That is precisely what personal prayer is all about, isn't it? It's taking the most intimate, the most precious, the most personal aspects of our life, the most threatening concerns that we have ever faced, and spreading them out before the Lord. "Look at this, Lord. Look at what I'm facing. Look, Lord, at what I'm up against."

Notice the dynamics at work here as Hezekiah spread his problems before the Lord. Here in his experience we find a good formula for handling bad news, impossible problems, and difficult people. Look at how it worked.

First, Hezekiah Humbled Himself

The Scriptures tell us that Hezekiah "tore his clothing" and covered himself with sackcloth (2 Kings 19:1). Biblically, that is a sign of humility, of inadequacy, of need, and of penitence. In humility, he comes to God for help.

Bob Zuppke was the football coach at Illinois back when the legendary Knute Rockne was the coach at Notre Dame. Like Rockne, Bob Zuppke was a master at the halftime pep talk. Some thought Zuppke was even better. At one particular game, Illinois had not played well at all in the first half, and at the halftime break they were way behind. Coach Zuppke knew he had to give one of his most dramatic speeches to fire up his dispirited squad.

And he did. As he neared the conclusion of his inspiring halftime pep talk, his voice became louder, his pleas became more dramatic, and finally, he pointed to the door at the other end of the locker room, saying, "And now let's go through that door and on to victory!" Then, the players were so moved, so inspired, so fired up that the team rose as one, tears welling in their eyes, throats choked with emotion, and they ran through that door—right into the university swimming pool! It was a humbling experience; they were going the wrong way.

Every now and then, we have to come in humility to God to get a sense of direction. It's interesting to note that this is a basic premise of Alcoholics Anonymous. To get help, you must come in humility, admitting, confessing that you have a problem and that you need help.

To get help from God, first of all, we have to humble ourselves. That's what Hezekiah did that day. First, he humbled himself.

Second, He Came to the Church

We are living today in a strangely individualistic society. Great emphasis is being put on individualism. The prevailing mottos are, "Do your own thing"; "Be your own person"; "Toot your own horn."

Occasionally, in that same vein I hear people say, "I can experience God anywhere. I don't have to go to a church. I can pray to God out on the lake or under a tree." Of course you can! God is everywhere. But let me tell you something with all the feeling I have in my heart: We need the church. I love the way Harry Emerson Fosdick put it. He said,

> Have you ever been in areas on this planet where no Christian church has ever been? I have. Ideas and spiritual values which we take for granted had never touched those areas. I could acutely feel the vacuum. And when I returned home, I almost wept when I saw the first church steeple. . . . I wish I had more than one life to give to the church. (Fosdick, *Dear Mr. Brown* [New York: Harper, 1961], 133-54)

Hezekiah came (as millions after him have come) in times of trouble to the altar of the church, to share his problems with the ministers there and with fellow believers there, and they encouraged him. If you have problems, if you have bad news, if you have to deal with difficult people, then let your church help you; let your Christian friends help you; claim the strength and support of the church community. Going it alone will only lead to misery and disaster. No one of us is an island. We all need a support group. We all need the church.

First, Hezekiah humbled himself. And second, he came to the church.

Third and Finally, He Reviewed His Problem Specifically with God and Trusted God to See Him through It

Some weeks ago, a man came to see me. It was late afternoon. His mother had died early that morning, and he had come by the church to talk about the funeral arrangements. As we visited, he told me about a poignant experience he had had earlier in the day. He was on his way to the funeral home, numb with grief, when he stopped for a traffic light just before a highway onramp. The traffic on the highway was zipping along. Cars were moving swiftly to the south and to the north. Horns were honking, trucks were roaring, tires were squealing, the sounds of traffic and busyness and life were going on.

At that moment, he had a strange feeling. He said he felt a sudden urge to jump out of his car and to scream at the traffic: "*Stop!* My mother died today! Stop! Don't you care?" Then he said to me, "Wasn't that silly? Wasn't that ridiculous? I knew those people couldn't stop, but somehow I wanted someone to stop and notice that this morning my mother died." "No," I said to him, "it's not silly at all to feel that way because someone doesn't stop. But God stops. God notices. God cares. That's the good news of our faith. God is with you, and he will see you through."

Hezekiah brought the specifics of his problem to God. He talked it out with God. There is great healing in that. Hezekiah trusted God, and in this instance, help came quickly. The Assyrians were turned back. Sennacherib was done in by his own sons. Jerusalem was saved. But even if the Assyrians had destroyed Jerusalem, the main thing to remember is that they could not destroy God.

So no matter what happens, no matter what problems come, the point is clear: those who stand with God cannot lose. Ultimately, the truth wins. Ultimately, love wins. Ultimately, God wins.

There is a powerful scene in Par Lagerkvist's novel *Barabbas* in which the Christian Sahak is brought before the emperor, and he is told to deny his Lord, to curse Christ. Sahak says, "I cannot do that." The emperor replies, "Don't you know that I can take away all your powers? Don't you know that I can take away all your freedom? Don't you know that I can take away your life?" "Yes," Sahak responds, "but you cannot take away my God."

No one can take away our God. When we have to face bad news, impossible problems, and difficult people, it helps if we remember that.

CHAPTER TWELVE

Remember the Strength of Sanctified Stubbornness

SCRIPTURE: PHILIPPIANS 1:12-21

Is stubbornness ever a virtue? The truth is that we do not usually include stubbornness on our list of virtuous qualities. Quite to the contrary, we most often list it as a vice, equating it with closed-mindedness or mule-headedness. If the symbol of peace is the descending dove, then the symbol of stubbornness would be the balking mule.

Have you heard about the man and his wife who, while on an automobile trip, got into a large-sized fuss over a small-sized incident? Neither would budge; neither would listen; neither of them would give an inch. Each loudly and stubbornly argued for his or her position, with neither giving in nor backing down. The heated debate was followed by a cold, stony silence. For miles they didn't speak to each other. Finally, they passed a pasture where a young farm boy was trying to pull a long-eared mule across a narrow, makeshift bridge. The mule balked; he would not budge an inch. The boy was pulling with all his might, but the mule was not about to move. The mule had dug in his heels. Seeing this scene, the man in the car broke the silence. "Look at that stubborn old mule!" he said. Then, pointing to the mule, he asked his wife, "Is that stubborn old mule a relative of yours?" The wife retorted, "Yes, on my husband's side!"

This is a light treatment of the heavy notion that we have about stubbornness, namely, that stubbornness usually does not make a pretty picture. Most often, stubbornness is narrow, rigid, arrogant, unyielding, prideful, unbending, difficult to live with, hard to handle. In Webster's dictionary, a synonym for *stubborn* is *obstinate*, which means "an unreasonable adherence to an opinion." That is the portrait of stubbornness we are most familiar with, isn't it? However, in one of the most fascinating and refreshing sections in all the Scriptures, the apostle Paul shows us in his letter to the Philippians that there is also a virtuous kind of stubbornness—a "sanctified stubbornness," a consecrated, tenacious determination to hold on and persevere no matter how dark and dismal the circumstances.

Paul was in prison in ill health, facing death, separated from his loved ones, cut off from his dream to take his ministry to Spain. To make matters worse, his opponents were ridiculing him, having a field day over his imprisonment. "Look at Paul's predicament," they chided. "Look what a fix he is in! Where is his God now? Don't listen to him anymore; follow us. We are the leaders you can count on, not him."

How did Paul respond to this terrible situation? Did he throw in the towel? Did he give up? Did he shake his fist at heaven? Did he curse God and die? No, Paul did none of these. Rather, with sanctified stubbornness he wrote, "I want you to know, brethren, that what has happened to me has really served to advance the gospel, so that it has become known throughout the whole praetorian guards and to all the rest that my imprisonment is for Christ; and most of the brethren have been made confident in the Lord because of my imprisonment, and are much more bold to speak the word of God without fear" (Philippians 1:12-14 RSV). This was Paul's Christian stubbornness breaking through, his unwavering dedication, his tenacious determination.

There are several interesting elements in this special brand of commitment.

Notice First That Paul Stubbornly Refused to Give in to Self-Pity

Notice the manner in which Paul spoke of his troubles: "What has happened to me ..." He did not wallow in self-pity; no dreary details. He did not weary his friends with a long-winded gloomy rehearsal of his hardships, problems, and misfortunes. He did not go around buttonholing people, making them listen to a long series of sad complaints.

How we need to learn a lesson from Paul! How quick we are to feel sorry for ourselves and to go on and on about our troubles. So often we are like the man filling out an application for work. When he came to the question, "Who should we notify if you get injured?" he wrote, "Anybody in sight!" How like that we often are—quick to give in to self-pity and quick to tell anybody in sight all the gory details. And how often we are like the woman whom you dare not ask, "How are you?" because she will tell you; in agonizing detail, she will tell you.

Not so with Paul. He simply referred to all his troubles as "what has happened to me." Interestingly, the New English Bible gives it a lighthearted and almost nonchalant turn of phrase: "Friends, I want you to understand that the work of the Gospel has been helped on, rather than hindered, by this 'business of mine.'" Imagine a man on the gallows, about to be hanged, referring to the rope as this "business of mine." Yet, Paul conveys exactly that spirit. He wrote with the courage of one who says, "This is the way things are and now we will get that over in a hurry and pass on to something really important." It is always inspiring to find someone who, though in miserable circumstances, stubbornly refuses to give in to self-pity and instead, dismisses their misery as "this business of mine."

Some years ago, Sir William Osier was walking through a hospital ward with one of his colleagues, Dr. Walsh. Osier told his friend that he wanted to introduce him to a rather remarkable medical case, a courageous patient. The patient was Sir William Osier's mother. At her bedside, this conversation took place.

"Mother, I would like for you to tell Dr. Walsh something of your life. When were you first in the hospital?"

"At age 27," she replied.

"What was the matter?"

"I had sarcoma of the right knee."

"What did they do for you?"

"They cut off the right leg at the hip."

"Did you get entirely well?"

"Yes, entirely well."

"When were you in again?" Dr. Osier continued.

"At age 42."

"What was the matter?"

"I had cancer of the chest and left shoulder."

"What did they do for you?"

"They removed part of the left shoulder and amputated the left arm."

"Did you get entirely well?"

"Yes, entirely well."

"What are you in the hospital for now?"

"For rheumatism." Then, catching the doctor's hand, she added, "I hope you will make me well in a hurry because I have to go home and take care of my grandchildren."

Stubbornness is a virtue when it is that indomitable spirit which enables us to refuse to give in to self-pity.

Second, Notice That Paul Stubbornly Refused to Be Shaken by Criticism

Paul refused to be daunted by criticism. We are so vulnerable on this point. We all want to be liked and respected. We want social approval. Even though we know that criticism is the device of small minds and little people, it still hurts us.

Paul was being criticized, ridiculed, laughed at. He felt the scoffers' jealousy, their envy, their resentment, but even in this weakened condition, he would not fold, would not break, would not come down to their level.

We see in Paul something of the spirit of Nehemiah. The Jewish people have returned to Jerusalem after the exile, and Nehemiah begins the arduous task of rebuilding the walls of Jerusalem. It seems such a hopeless job—the people scattered, discouraged, despondent; but Nehemiah builds on, laying brick after brick on that wall. His enemies tease and taunt him, they ridicule and criticize him, even threaten him; but Nehemiah has the perfect answer: "I'm doing a great work and I cannot come down" (Nehemiah 6:3). That's the spirit of Paul.

When you have found your task, made your commitment, discovered your purpose; when you know in your heart what you must say and do and be, you are then pretty well immune from either the praise or blame of people. Whether the crowd around you is flinging bouquets to you or slinging mud on you makes little difference, because you are doing a great work and you can't come down. When the word came to Paul that some were preaching out of envy and rivalry and were criticizing him, he responded with a spirit of bigness: "So what? It doesn't matter what they say about me. All that matters is that Christ is proclaimed, and in that I rejoice."

Third, Paul Stubbornly Refused to Quit

Paul would not fold up his tent, he would not lose hope. He even saw good things coming out of his misfortunes. God was turning defeats into victories.

How could this be? Paul was chained to a Roman

guard. How could good come from that? Well, Paul saw it as a unique opportunity. He wrote words that became scripture, words that have touched the hearts of people all over the world.

Not only that, he had the unique opportunity to preach to some of the most influential people in the Roman Empire. "Sure I'm trapped here," Paul said, "but don't you see, it's really a blessing in disguise, because people are hearing about Christ who never heard of him before." According to historians, Paul was chained by wrist or ankle to a member of the elite praetorian guard, and every four hours the guard would change, which meant for Paul that every four hours he had chained to him a captive congregation. And such a congregation—the emperor's personal bodyguards, the most fashionable, exclusive, and influential regiment of soldiers in Rome. Paul saw this not as a place to quit, but as a special, unique opportunity.

Also, fellow Christians were greatly inspired as they saw firsthand how Paul conducted himself under pressure. As they saw him in action, they became more courageous and more committed. It didn't happen automatically. It happened because of something in the character and attitude of Paul.

We see here, once again, that it is not so much what happens to us; rather, it is how we respond to what happens to us. Paul not only made the best of a bad situation, he made the most of it.

Fourth and Finally, Notice That Paul Stubbornly Refused to Compromise on His Commitment to God

Paul kept on trusting God, even in the darkest hour. Though times were tough, he tenaciously hung on to his faith in God. He was in prison, he was in ill health, he was separated from his loved ones, cut off from his dream; he was being severely criticized, and he was facing death. But despite all of that, he did not waver, he did not bend, he did not rail against heaven, he did not compromise on his commitments to God. He kept on holding to what was right, kept on believing the best, kept on trusting God. Remember how Paul put it: "For me to live is Christ, and to die is gain" (Philippians 1:21 RSV).

I want to encourage you to see the Academy Award-winning Best Picture of 1981, *Chariots of Fire*. It is the story of Eric Liddell's consecrated stubbornness, his stubborn refusal to compromise his principles. Eric Liddell was born in China, the son of Christian missionaries from Scotland. Back in Scotland for his education, Liddell became one of Scotland's most distinguished and respected athletes, first as a rugby player and later as a sprinter. The missionary society sensed his unique abilities as a runner, and they encouraged him to train for the Olympic Games. "We need some muscular Christians," they said to him. "Your athletic achievements will enhance your witness and open doors for you to proclaim your message. You, Eric Liddell, must run—not for personal glory, but to honor God."

So Eric Liddell ran; with reckless abandon he ran. Every day he ran, except Sunday. He never ran or trained on Sunday because that is God's day; he had been taught that from youth.

He became the greatest sprinter in Scotland and was selected to run the 100-meter dash for the United Kingdom in the Olympic Games held in Paris that year. However, en route to Paris, primed and ready, Eric Liddell heard something that just couldn't be true, but it was: the qualifying heat for the 100-meter dash was scheduled to be run on Sunday. Eric Liddell wanted, more than we can imagine, to run in the Olympic Games, but he refused to run. He refused to compromise his principles, he refused to water down his commitment, he refused to rationalize his conscience. To run on Sunday would have been for him a contradiction of what he was there for, because he was there to honor God.

The qualifying heat was indeed held on Sunday, and

Eric Liddell stubbornly refused to run. But if you look at the Olympic records, you will find the name of Eric Liddell. He ran later in the week in the 400 meter dash, a race he had not trained for and previously had not competed in at an international competition. He not only won but also he set a new Olympic record. Later he became a missionary to China.

Eric Liddell is remembered not because he won an Olympic race, but because he, like Paul, stubbornly refused to compromise in his commitment to God. Eric Liddell joined a great line of committed people who became a great inspiration to the world because they stubbornly refused to compromise on their commitment to God. There was Peter, saying boldly, "We must obey God rather than men" (Acts 5:29 RSV). There was Jesus, saying in the Garden of Gethsemane, "Father, . . . not my will, but thine, be done" (Luke 22:42 RSV). And there was Paul, saying, "For me to live is Christ, and to die is gain" (Philippians 1:21 RSV). Yes, stubbornness can be a virtue, when it enables us to rise above self-pity; to rise above criticism; to rise above quitting when times are tough, and when the world takes the wind out of our sails; and to rise above compromising on our commitment to God.

DISCUSSION GUIDE

for
When the World Takes the Wind Out of Your Sails

BY JOHN D. SCHROEDER

1. Remember That Our Hope Is in God

Snapshot Summary

This chapter looks at the importance of hope and a strong faith in God when we face the storms of life.

Reflection/Discussion Questions

1. Share your interest in this book and what you hope to gain from your experience of reading and discussing it.
2. Share a time in your life when you battled a storm and needed to have hope.
3. What impresses you most about the miracle story in Mark 4?
4. Give an example from personal experience of how life is uncertain.
5. How can building a strong faith prepare you for life's storms?
6. If you knew a storm or crisis was coming tomorrow, what would you do today?

7. In your own words, what does it mean to have hope in God?
8. Describe some times in life when people need hope.
9. How can we help others when they experience one of life's storms?
10. What additional thoughts or ideas from this chapter would you like to explore?

Activities

As a group: Search the Bible for messages about hope. Use index cards and markers to create affirmations of hope in God, to serve as a reminder in troubled times. Share your affirmations with one another.

At home: Offer hope this week to someone who needs it.

Prayer: *Dear God, thank you for being with us during the storms of life. Help us build a strong faith to prepare us for the rough spots. Amen.*

2. Remember That with God's Help You Can Bounce Back

Snapshot Summary

This chapter explores how to recover from a broken heart by talking it out, working it out, and seeking God's help to bounce back.

Reflection/Discussion Questions

1. Share a time when you had your heart broken. How did you cope?
2. Describe some of the different ways people react to terrible news.

3. How does it feel to have your heart broken? Give some descriptive adjectives.
4. Why does it help to talk it out? Name some of the benefits.
5. If your heart was broken, who would you talk to, and why?
6. Name some ways people "work it out."
7. How can the church be part of the healing process?
8. Describe some of the ways God helps us bounce back.
9. Reflect on / discuss how to help someone who has just experienced heartbreak.
10. What additional thoughts or ideas from this chapter would you like to explore?

Activities

As a Group: If you were making a first-aid kit for a broken heart, what would it contain? Make a list of essential items and share your results.

At Home: Pray daily this week for someone, known or unknown, who is experiencing a broken heart and is in need of healing.

Prayer: *Dear God, thank you for being there for us when we are down and for helping us bounce back when we are broken. Help us seek the help we need in times of trouble and believe in brighter days ahead. Amen.*

3. Remember That It Is Important to Push Out of the Shallows

Snapshot Summary

This chapter reminds us of the need to experience depth in our lives, to express gratitude for what we have, to offer penitence, and to deepen our commitment to God.

Reflection/Discussion Questions

1. What impressed you about the story of the church that was $14,000 short of its goal?
2. Reflect on / discuss what it means to "push out of the shallows." How is this done?
3. Share a time when you were tired and ready to quit, but gave it one more try.
4. Give some reasons why it is important to launch out into the deep. What are the benefits?
5. Reflect on / discuss different ways gratitude can be expressed.
6. Share a time when you felt extremely grateful for an unexpected blessing.
7. Give your own definition of penitence, and share an example of it.
8. Describe some ways to deepen your commitment to God and to others.
9. Name some tools that can help you leave the shallows and experience depth in life.
10. What additional thoughts or ideas from this chapter would you like to explore?

Activities

As a Group: Let each member write a brief prayer based upon the message of this chapter. Share your prayers.

At Home: Examine your own life and look for areas where greater depth is needed. Try to push out of the shallows in one area of your life this week.

Prayer: *Dear God, thank you for encouraging us to go deeper into life and experience more of what life offers. Help us remember and express gratitude for all our blessings and deepen our commitment to you and to others. Amen.*

4. Remember That There Is Amazing Power in the Cross

Snapshot Summary

This chapter shows us how the cross is a powerful reminder of God's love for us, and a symbol for how God wants us to live our lives in a Christlike way.

Reflection/Discussion Questions

1. What words and images come to mind when you reflect upon the amazing power of the cross?
2. "God does much of his best work through regular folks"; give an example of this from your own life or your own observations.
3. Why are we often tempted to grab for the crown rather than take the way of the cross?
4. Name some Christlike values that all Christians should seek and cultivate.
5. How does Jesus define success?
6. What happens when we accept Christ into our lives? How are we changed?
7. Explain what it means to take up the cross of Christlike love.
8. Share a time when someone offered Christlike love to you.
9. Reflect on / discuss different ways in which Christians can increase Christlike commitment.
10. What additional thoughts or ideas from this chapter would you like to explore?

Activities

As a Group: Search the Bible for references and insights to the amazing power of the cross. Share and discuss your findings.

At Home: Reflect daily upon the symbol of the cross, what it means to you, and the hope it provides.

Prayer: *Dear God, thank you for all that you have given to us through the cross of Christ. Help us be more Christlike in all that we say and do. Amen.*

5. Remember That We Can Trust God and Go Forward

Snapshot Summary

This chapter examines the trust Moses had in God and the different reactions people have when faced with a roadblock in life.

Reflection/Discussion Questions

1. Share a time when you trusted God and then went forward.
2. What impresses you most about how Moses trusted God?
3. Give some reasons why "to go back to where we were" has great appeal. What is wrong about this approach?
4. Why is "the past" a powerful influence in decision-making?
5. Share a time when you wanted to run away and hide but didn't. What did you do instead?
6. Describe some of the dangers of self-pity.
7. Why is it tempting to blame others for our problems?
8. Why can we always trust God?
9. How does God want us to respond to trouble?
10. What additional thoughts or ideas from this chapter would you like to explore?

Activities

As a Group: Search a hymnal or songbook for insights about trusting God.

At Home: Select a particular problem or situation in your life this week, and make a commitment to trust God and move forward toward resolution.

Prayer: *Dear God, thank you for the reminder that we can trust you and then move forward knowing you are with us. Help us avoid self-pity and blaming others. Instead of running away and trying to hide, help us run to you. Amen.*

6. Remember That Easter Has Good News for You

Snapshot Summary

This chapter reminds us of the good news of Easter and the strength, power, and comfort it offers every day.

Reflection/Discussion Questions

1. Share how your view of Easter has changed over the years, from when you were a child to adulthood.
2. Can you recall when you first heard the biblical Easter story or who shared it with you? Give details as you can recall them.
3. In your own words, what does Easter mean to you?
4. Reflect on / discuss the comfort and consolation Easter offers.
5. Tell of a Good Friday experience in your life where life threatened to do you in and bury you.
6. What does it mean to take up Jesus' ministry of sacrificial love?
7. Reflect on / discuss some of the types of work ministry opportunities available to Christians.
8. Describe the companionship that the Holy Spirit offers.
9. How should Easter be observed and celebrated?
10. What additional thoughts or ideas from this chapter would you like to explore?

Activities

As a Group: Use art supplies to create messages and illustrations of the good news of Easter. Share your creations.

At Home: Celebrate the gifts of Easter all week. Read the Easter story again and meditate upon it. Reflect upon how your life and future has changed because of Christ's death on the cross and his resurrection.

Prayer: *Dear God, thank you for the good news of Easter and the message of hope it contains all year long. Help us live with joy and thanksgiving because of Jesus. Amen.*

7. Remember That the Holy Spirit Is with You

Snapshot Summary

This chapter reminds us how the Holy Spirit ministers to us and how Pentecost gives us a new way of looking at Christ. It also examines the role Simon Peter played in the Pentecost story.

Reflection/Discussion Questions

1. Reflect on / discuss why Jesus sent the Holy Spirit. How does the Holy Spirit help us?
2. What impresses you the most about the Pentecost story?
3. Describe the role Simon Peter played in Pentecost.
4. Why do we need a new way of looking at the world?
5. "Pentecost gives us the eyes of love and inclusiveness"; why is this important?
6. Share a time when you were cut to the heart like Simon Peter.
7. Why do we all need a new way of looking at ourselves?
8. How does Pentecost give us a new way of looking at Christ? Why is this important?

9. What do we need to do in order to receive the Holy Spirit?
10. What additional thoughts or ideas from this chapter would you like to explore?

Activities

As a Group: Let each group member make a list of what Pentecost and the Holy Spirit teach us. Share your findings.

At Home: Reflect on ways you can invite the Holy Spirit to fill your life.

Prayer: *Dear God, thank you for your gift of the Holy Spirit. When the world takes the wind out of our sails, may the Holy Spirit breathe upon us, calm us, and restore us. Amen.*

8. Remember That the Spiritual Disciplines Do Work

Snapshot Summary

This chapter examines how the spiritual disciplines transform lives and why we need them today.

Reflection/Discussion Questions

1. Share what alarms you most about what is happening in the world today.
2. Do you believe we face worse problems today than those faced by earlier generations? Explain.
3. What is the discipline of worship, and why is it important?
4. Why are many people inattentive to spiritual matters?
5. Share some of the benefits you receive from regular worship.

6. Reflect on / discuss what it means to practice the discipline of trust, to really trust God.
7. Describe some ways we can show our trust in God.
8. How do we pass along to others the discipline of love?
9. Who helped you "sing Christ's song of love"? Who made Christ's love real to you?
10. What additional thoughts or ideas from this chapter would you like to explore?

Activities

As a Group: Talk about the importance of having discipline in the different aspects of your life. Make a list of ideas and encouragements for living a more disciplined life.

At Home: Take an inventory of the spiritual disciplines. In which are you the strongest in your life, and in which are you the weakest? Which spiritual discipline needs the most work in your life? Decide how to make necessary improvements.

Prayer: *Dear God, thank you for the spiritual disciplines that help us live happy, healthy, and productive lives. Help us become more disciplined in spiritual matters and place greater importance upon them. Amen.*

9. Remember That There Is Help Available

Snapshot Summary

This chapter examines the problem of stress and shows us how God and others can help us find peace and relief.

Reflection/Discussion Questions

1. Share a time when you were stressed and how you dealt with it.
2. What does stress feel like? What are some symptoms of

stress? How do you personally know when you are stressed?

3. Name some common causes of stress.
4. What are some of the dangers of long-term stress?
5. Reflect on / discuss why Moses was stressed, and what he did about it.
6. Why is it smart to turn to your friends when stressed? How can they help?
7. What help does the church offer in times of stress?
8. Name some ways God can help you when you are stressed.
9. Why do some people try and carry the burden alone when they are stressed?
10. What additional thoughts or ideas from this chapter would you like to explore?

Activities

As a Group: Locate and share Bible verses that calm you and provide stress relief.

At Home: Reread this chapter and make a reminder list of the help and ideas it provides. When you find yourself stressed this week, remember these ideas and seek to put them into practice in your life.

Prayer: *Dear God, thank you providing us with calm when we are stressed. Help us not take things more seriously than we should, and help us trust in you more. Amen.*

10. Remember to Pray in the Spirit of Christ

Snapshot Summary

This chapter reminds us of the power of prayer and shows us Christlike ways to pray in the spirit of Christ.

Reflection/Discussion Questions

1. What misunderstandings have you seen concerning prayer?
2. Reflect on / discuss what Jesus said about prayer, and how the manner in which he prayed.
3. According to the author, what is the key to a meaningful prayer life?
4. Explain what it means to "be in the spirit of Christ" when you pray.
5. Give an example of asking God to bless us at the expense of others. Why is it not OK to do this?
6. What is the Christlike way to ask God for forgiveness?
7. When we pray for others, what is the Christlike way to do so?
8. When we ask God in prayer to help us, how should we pray?
9. Why is it important to pray for God's will to be done?
10. What additional thoughts or ideas from this chapter would you like to explore?

Activities

As a Group: Let each member of the group write a brief prayer that is in the spirit of Christ. Share what you have written.

At Home: Reflect upon your prayer life. What would you like to improve upon?

Prayer: *Dear God, thank you for the ability to communicate with you through the power of prayer. Help us remember to keep in contact with you throughout each day. Amen.*

11. Remember That You Can Spread Your Problems Before the Lord

Snapshot Summary

This chapter uses the story of Hezekiah to show how to handle bad news, impossible problems, and difficult people.

Reflection/Discussion Questions

1. Share what you have learned about handling problems as you have grown older.
2. Describe what you think are the worst types of problems.
3. What impressed you about Hezekiah and how he handled his problems?
4. In your own words, what does it mean to be humble? How do you humble yourself before God?
5. What help does the church offer troubled people?
6. Hezekiah "brought the specifics of his problem to God." Why is this important?
7. Why is trusting God an important element of problem solving?
8. What are some of the worst things you can do with a problem?
9. Name some ways we can help others with the problems they face.
10. What additional thoughts or ideas from this chapter would you like to explore?

Activities

As a Group: Spend five minutes silently praying about your problems or the problems of others. At the end of the five minutes, give participants the opportunity to offer a brief comment on how it feels to give your problems to God.

At Home: Present one or two of your biggest problems to God in prayer, then work with God during the week to make progress toward dealing with them or solving them.

Prayer: *Dear God, thank you for caring about our problems and for always being there to help us in times of trouble. Remind us of the power of prayer to change lives and situations. Amen.*

12. Remember the Strength of Sanctified Stubbornness

Snapshot Summary

This chapter uses the life of the apostle Paul to illustrate situations where it is good and proper to be stubborn.

Reflection/Discussion Questions

1. Share a time when you acted in a stubborn manner.
2. In your own words, what does it mean to be stubborn?
3. Reflect on / discuss the apostle Paul's stubbornness, and why he acted in that manner.
4. Why is it a virtue not to give in to self-pity?
5. Why is it easy to be shaken by criticism? Can stubbornness help? Explain.
6. Reflect on / discuss how God can turn defeats into victories if we refuse to quit.
7. What does it mean to refuse to compromise on your commitment to God?
8. How do you know if your stubbornness is productive (good) or non-productive (bad)?
9. Why do we need to be stubborn about our beliefs and values? How can this be achieved?
10. What additional thoughts or ideas from this chapter would you like to explore?

Activities

As a Group: Have an informal graduation party to mark the conclusion of your reading of this book and your group discussion.

At Home: Reflect upon what you have gained in your reading, reflection, and discussion, and where you want to go from here.

Prayer: *Dear God, thank you for showing us the good aspects of stubbornness and when it is appropriate to stand firm. Thank you for the people of this group and our time together. Be with us as we go our separate ways. Amen.*